Philosophy
After Deleuze

DELEUZE ENCOUNTERS

Series Editor: Ian Buchanan, Professor and Director of the Institute for Social Transformation and Research, University of Wollongong, Australia.

The *Deleuze Encounters* series provides students in philosophy and related subjects with concise and accessible introductions to the application of Deleuze's work in key areas of study. Each book demonstrates how Deleuze's ideas and concepts can enhance present work in a particular field.

Series titles include:

Cinema After Deleuze, Richard Rushton
Political Theory After Deleuze, Nathan Widder
Theology After Deleuze, Kristien Justaert
Space After Deleuze, Arun Saldanha

Philosophy After Deleuze

Deleuze and the Genesis of Representation II

JOE HUGHES

BLOOMSBURY
LONDON · NEW DELHI · NEW YORK · SYDNEY

Bloomsbury Academic
An imprint of Bloomsbury Publishing Plc

50 Bedford Square	175 Fifth Avenue
London	New York
WC1B 3DP	NY 10010
UK	USA

www.bloomsbury.com

First published 2012

© Joe Hughes, 2012

All rights reserved. No part of this publication may be reproduced or transmitted in any form or by any means, electronic or mechanical, including photocopying, recording, or any information storage or retrieval system, without prior permission in writing from the publishers.

Joe Hughes has asserted his right under the Copyright, Designs and Patents Act, 1988, to be identified as Author of this work.

No responsibility for loss caused to any individual or organization acting on or refraining from action as a result of the material in this publication can be accepted by Bloomsbury Academic or the author.

British Library Cataloguing-in-Publication Data
A catalogue record for this book is available from the British Library.

ISBN: HB: 978-1-4411-4715-8
PB: 978-1-4411-9516-6

Library of Congress Cataloging-in-Publication Data
Hughes, Joe.
Philosophy after Deleuze/Joe Hughes.
p. cm. – (Deleuze encounters)
Includes bibliographical references (p.) and index.
ISBN 978-1-4411-4715-8 (hardcover) – ISBN 978-1-4411-9516-6 (pbk.) –
ISBN 978-1-4411-8798-7 (ebook (epub)) – ISBN 978-1-4411-9154-0 (ebook (pdf))
1. Deleuze, Gilles, 1925–1995. I. Title.

B2430.D454H845 2012
194–dc23

2012007521

Typeset by Deanta Global Publishing Services, Chennai, India

To Winifred

Contents

Acknowledgments viii
List of abbreviations ix

1 Style 1
2 Ontology 27
3 Ethics 57
4 Aesthetics 79
5 Politics 113

Notes 147
Bibliography 167
Index 173

Acknowledgments

A lot of people have helped me out with specific problems, talked me off of certain ledges, and obliquely suggested paths I actually took. I owe particular thanks to Maria Damon for talking me into writing this, and to Ian Buchanan for talking me into writing it twice. Much of what is written here has been shaped by conversations with friends, colleagues, and the wonderful Deleuze studies community (if you could call it that). In particular . . . Young-ok An, Jeff Bell, Nadine Boljkovac, Ray Brassier, Tony Brown, Levi Bryant, Cesare Casarino, Claire Colebrook, Felicity Colman, Moira Gatens, Christian Haines, Hyeryung Hwang, Wim Ibes, Sabrina Jaromin, Eleanor Kaufman, Wim Kok, Simon Malpas, Matt McGuire, Andrew Marzoni, Mike Olson, Jay Nombalais, Paul Patton, Patricia Pisters, John Protevi, Kevin Riordan, Matthias Rothe, Dan Selcer, Dan Smith, Robb St. Lawrence, Kenneth Surin, Paul Tiensuu, Kiarina Kordela, Annemarie Lawless, and William Watkin. Thanks always to Sarah Tukua.

List of abbreviations

Deleuze and Guattari:

AO	*Anti-Oedipus*
ATP	*A Thousand Plateaus*
BG	*Bergsonism*
C1	*Cinema 1*
C2	*Cinema 2*
DI	*Desert Islands*
DR	*Difference and Repetition*
EC	*Essays Critical and Clinical*
EP	*Expressionism in Philosophy*
ES	*Empiricism and Subjectivity*
FB	*Francis Bacon*
FC	*Foucault*
I&I	*Instincts et institutions*
KA	*Kafka*
KCP	*Kant's Critical Philosophy*
LS	*The Logic of Sense*
NP	*Nietzsche and Philosophy*
PI	*Pure Immanence*
PS	*Proust and Signs*

LIST OF ABBREVIATIONS

SPP *Spinoza: Practical Philosophy*
TF   *The Fold*
WP   *What is Philosophy?*

Other authors:

CJ   Kant, *Critique of Judgment*
CPR Kant, *Critique of Pure Reason*
CPr Kant, *Critique of Practical Reason*
MM   Bergson, *Matter and Memory*

1

Style

What is striking is that in literature deceit and mystification not only are inevitable but constitute the writer's honesty, whatever hope and truth are in him. . . . Naturally, a writer can always make it his ideal to call a cat a cat. But what he cannot manage to do is then believe that he is on the way to health and sincerity.[1]

What characterizes the signs of human language is not so much their generality as their mobility.[2]

Deleuze is a difficult writer. His first challenge to his readers is textual rather than philosophical, and the decisions we make about how to deal with this difficulty determine in advance the kinds of things we say about Deleuze's thought. The central argument of this book is that Deleuze's philosophy is best understood as a reconfiguration of Kant's. But before that claim can be made, and in order for it to have its maximum extension, it is necessary first of all to come to terms with Deleuze's style. The most important characteristic of this style is the conceptual monotony which supports it. The aspect we are most consistently in denial about is his refusal to extend, to even (or especially) his most generous readers, a gesture of goodwill.

Goodwill

In the third chapter of *Difference and Repetition*, Deleuze sketches the outlines of a "new image of thought."[3] Most of *Difference and Repetition* is devoted to describing what this new thought is and explaining how it works in the world.[4] But before this new image can be described, and before the real work of the book can begin, Deleuze takes a series of methodological precautions by characterizing what he calls the "dogmatic image of thought."

If this older image of thought is dogmatic it is because it relies on a series of unstated presuppositions or "postulates" which uncritically determine the field of philosophy in advance. Deleuze identifies eight postulates, ranging from the assumption that thought is primarily propositional and, when in good form, logical, to presuppositions about the very unity of thought. About half of these were already developed in two earlier texts, *Nietzsche and Philosophy* (1962) and *Proust and Signs* (1964). Across all three texts, however, only one postulate remains constant: philosophy depends too heavily on the "*goodwill of the thinker.*"[5] It "assumes in advance the goodwill of thinking."[6]

Unlike the other postulates this one has as many implications for the writing and reading of philosophy as it does for Deleuze's concepts themselves. And even more unlike the others, this one seems like it's actually a good assumption to make and one that is worth upholding. Philosophy, or indeed any kind of textual communication, seems to require as its very condition the goodwill of the thinkers involved, and this goodwill has traditionally grounded an entire ethics of writing: do not be willfully obscure, do not manipulate source material, do not lie to your readers, mean what you say, and so on. What would communication without goodwill look like? And would it even be possible? My first argument here is that Deleuze's texts present us with this very image, and that this leads to at least two important consequences. (Whether or not this leads to a new way of *communicating* is an open question and depends entirely on whether you find my arguments in the remainder of this book persuasive.)

The first consequence is that we can no longer assume that the philosopher is our friend. Deleuze himself develops this most clearly in the second iteration of the postulate. In *Proust and Signs*, Deleuze writes that one of the central consequences of this presupposition is that we believe that

> in the "philosopher" there is a "friend" . . . Friends are, in relation to one another, like minds of goodwill who are in agreement as to the signification of things and words; they communicate under the effect of a mutual goodwill.[7]

We assume that when someone writes a text, they are writing it because they want us to understand it; and we, in turn, look past the minor blemishes and disagreements in order to understand what the writer was trying to tell us. Deleuze, however, overturns this relationship. In his texts, the philosopher becomes a "surly interlocutor,"[8] an interlocutor who writes not with a will to truth but with a "will to deceive."[9] Thought, Deleuze says, is not advanced at pleasant "dinner conversations at Mr. Rorty's;"[10] rather, we advance our thought in violent encounters which jolt and shock our former way of thinking. The implicit answer to the questions in title of the first chapter of *Dialogues*, "A Conversation: What is it? What is it for?," is "nothing." This leads to a first consequence of the postulate: we cannot trust Deleuze. We have to expect that far from writing with a goodwill, he is surly and deceptive.

Replacing the friend with the surly interlocutor has further implications than this, however. Notice the second half of his claim. It is even more striking. Friends are minds of goodwill who are in *agreement as to the signification of things and words*. The contrary situation—that we might not agree on the meanings of our words—raises the very real possibility that Deleuze's words do not mean what we think they mean. This obviously is not an absolute rule. Most of his words do mean what we think they mean, but some words do not, and the difficulty is not that all of his words break with their conventional meanings but that some do and that it is not easy to tell which words he is using conventionally and which meanings he is inverting. This is a second major consequence of Deleuze's new image of thought: we cannot assume that words mean what we think they mean.

I do not think we have taken this postulate—which remains consistent from Deleuze's second major text all the way to his last—seriously enough. It is easy to assume that Deleuze is directing this assumption at other readers—maybe analytic philosophers, maybe Jean-Jacques Lecercle's bespectacled yuppie in the Paris metro who accidently picked up *What is Philosophy?* But this postulate does not bear on these mostly imagined readers who probably do not get more than few pages into any one of Deleuze's texts. It bears primarily on us—people committed to reading Deleuze carefully. What changes would we have to make if we really acknowledged that his will is not a will toward clarity and truth, but a will to deceive?—that, to requote Blanchot, "deceit and mystification not only are inevitable but constitute the writer's honesty"?

This affirmation of deception and refusal of goodwill is grounded in Deleuze's philosophy. If the rejection of this postulate disrupts both the possibility of sociable communication and the very meaning of words, it is because it has a much broader target: it disrupts the reliance of communication on opinion and convention. "Minds communicate to each other only the conventional,"[11] Deleuze writes in *Proust and Signs*, "only the conventional is explicit."[12] Direct, honest discourse, and the clarity we hope it brings, relies on conventions. And if we understand by convention those habits of making meaning which become naturalized over time, it is hard to dispute this point—but it is also hard to see why Deleuze would want to overturn it. What is wrong with convention?

To answer this question it is necessary to anticipate the arguments I will develop over the next couple of chapters. The heart of Deleuze's philosophy is the moment at which our "reactivity," our "passivity" or our "sensory-motor" habits fail. They become inadequate to a certain situation and we are confronted with the necessity of becoming creative, of finding an adequate reaction to the situation at hand. It is in this failure of habit that our power of thinking, the "virtual," is awakened and creates an Idea adequate to the situation. If Deleuze is interested in challenging convention, then, it is not because conventions are categorically bad and ought to be done away with for good. It is, rather, because when we communicate by convention, we are not yet thinking. Conventions are habits of producing meaning. They are the operations we perform on a text in the blink of an eye, without realizing we have done anything at all, and which transform the words into a basic sense. Deleuze's prose style is designed to engineer the basic failure of our reading habits. This failure is not a dead end, however. Rather, it forces us to take on new ways of reading and develop new habits adequate to his texts. Thus, in reading Deleuze, we are subject to an aesthetic education in which we live the new image of thought he describes philosophically. I will describe this new image of thought over the following chapters. For now, I want to emphasize that in overturning the postulate of goodwill, Deleuze's prose style forces us to give up a series of conventions. It's not just that the goodwill which is at the foundations of a whole ethics of writing is no longer operative, and it's not only that Deleuze might be willfully deceptive every now and then, the central difficulty here is that we cannot even be sure of the very signification of his words. At the same time, however, this forces us to take on new ways of reading: we need to read suspiciously, aware of Deleuze's will to deceive, and from the point of view of a linguistic indeterminacy in which the power of words is their mobility.

Indirection

One of the most obvious places in which Deleuze's unfriendliness is manifested is in his historical studies. Most of Deleuze's early books are about other philosophers: Hume, Nietzsche, Kant, Spinoza, and so on. In 1973, Michel Cressole wrote a letter to Deleuze accusing him of lingering in the "stuffy" and "smoke-filled halls" of a history of philosophy, the death of which Deleuze celebrated only after having "rewritten its history".[13] Deleuze famously replied with this:

> I myself 'did' history of philosophy for a long time, read books on this or that author. But I compensated in various ways . . . . But I suppose the main way I coped with it at the time was to see the history of philosophy as a sort of buggery (*enculage*) or (it comes to the same thing) immaculate conception. I saw myself as taking an author from behind and giving him a child that would be his own offspring, yet monstrous. It was really important for it to be his own child, because the author had to actually say all I had him saying. But the child was bound to be monstrous too, because it resulted from all sorts of shifting, slipping, dislocations, and hidden emissions that I really enjoyed.[14]

This is a particularly surly way of putting it—one which is partly justified by the context of the letter and his relationship to Cressole—but it captures an essential aspect of Deleuze's style, and that's its tendency toward free-indirect discourse, or, less technically, toward ventriloquism.

We often get the sense that rather than speaking *about* a certain philosopher, Deleuze is speaking *through* them. This is not to imply that there is anything directly and obviously mischievous going on in Deleuze's texts. His readings are often faithful and graceful and the whole rhetoric of violent encounters and ill will threatens to obscure this. (Deleuze is clear, after all, that the child of this encounter is still Nietzsche's or Bergson's own offspring.) What needs to be emphasized instead is that the emissions are hidden and the slippages are indirect. They take place through slight changes in emphasis, through novel coordinations, by shifting a marginal text to a place of prominence in an oeuvre, or by amplifying themes that are not entirely developed in the original material,[15] and so forth. Thus, while his readings remain faithful, there emerges a hazy, indeterminate sense of something distinctly Deleuzian. Foucault captures this effect brilliantly in his reading of *Difference and Repetition*:

> In the sentry box of the Luxemburg Gardens, Duns Scotus places his head through the circular window; he is sporting an impressive moustache; it belongs to Nietzsche, disguised as Klossowski.[16]

In this play of masks, the Deleuzian moment becomes very difficult to locate. Where is Deleuze in this assemblage? We might say that "Deleuze" is just that organizational force behind this odd synthesis of Klossowski, Nietzsche and Duns Scotus, but that does not get us very far in determining which concepts are specific to Deleuze and which to Klossowski. While Foucault was thinking of *Difference and Repetition*, this play of masks figures even more prominently in Deleuze's historical commentaries on Hume, Bergson, Nietzsche, and so on. This leads to a considerable problem: these texts, the bulk of Deleuze's oeuvre, give us some of our best insights into Deleuze's philosophical project, but in reading them, we never know who is talking.

This indirection—like his manipulation of convention—is tied to a central imperative of Deleuze's thought: to philosophize is to create concepts. Even in the letter to Cressole, Deleuze justified his ventriloquism by pointing toward the oppressive conditions of philosophy. By means of this buggery, Deleuze was able to say something new and in his own voice. This highlights an essential aspect of free-indirect philosophizing: it has the potential to become a form of positive creation. This is most explicit in his last major text, *What is Philosophy?*

> Nothing positive is done, nothing at all, in the domains of either criticism or history, when we are content to brandish ready-made concepts like skeletons intended to intimidate any creation, without seeing that the ancient philosophers from whom we borrow them were already doing what we would like to prevent modern philosophers from doing: they were inventing concepts, and they were not happy just to clean and scrape bones like the critic and historian of our time. Even the history of philosophy is completely without interest if it does not undertake to awaken a dormant concept and to play it again on a new stage, even if this comes at the price of turning it against itself.[17]

We can hear in this passage the famous claim of *What is Philosophy?* that philosophy is the creation of concepts. But this creation is not exclusively or even primarily a creation from nothing. Concepts are created by playing old concepts again on a new stage. We do not scrape the flesh off of the bones of history to finally get to an indubitable but ossified concept. We take the concept and bring it back to life in a new environment.

While this sounds great and liberating, we should dwell for a moment on the risk Deleuze mentions: in replaying concepts, we turn them against themselves, we distort their meanings, and we put them to work doing things they were never intended to do. We might draw two general consequences from this with respect to the question of Deleuze's style. What this means first of all is that the movement of a concept is not tied to its name which presumably remains constant even as the concept is turned against itself. Deleuze and Nietzsche can both talk of a "will to power" but mean different things (this will become more important below). There is a kind of loosening of the relation between concept and name. But even more importantly, to play a concept again on a new stage at risk of inverting its sense means that a Bergsonian, Nietzschean, or Kantian concept can become a Deleuzian concept without ever really indicating where the distinction between Deleuze and, say, Kant can be drawn. As Deleuze puts it in *Cinema II*, free-indirect discourse involves a "double-becoming."[18]

Critique

It is worth emphasizing here that this ventriloquism was by no means specific to Deleuze. Blanchot's claim that "in literature deceit and mystification not only are inevitable but constitute the writer's honesty," already indicates that Deleuze would find an ally in him. Blanchot regularly speaks "the falsity of all direct discourse,"[19] and what Deleuze does in his monographs, Blanchot had been doing across hundreds of book reviews since the early '30s. Blanchot's texts, whether they are on Mallarmé, Rilke, or Claudel—all come back to a finite and more or less consistent set of themes. Blanchot is an interesting figure here less because he can appear as an individual ally, however, but because of Blanchot's deep connections with Bataille's review *Critique*.[20]

To some extent, *Critique* institutionalized the free-indirect style (though this argument itself would require much more support than what I present here). This is in part due to the limits of the review-form.[21] As Michel Surya explains in his biography of Bataille, the journal was a "project offering a place to debate ideas by means of a critique of their transmission and circulation."[22] But there are only so many ways to advance one's own ideas in a review—especially if one of the advertised intentions of the review is to avoid "easy polemic"[23]— and to do so indirectly and without flagging your intervention is one of the most interesting. As Surya puts it, "*Critique* would not be a place of 'pure' ideas, or creation, but of critical commentaries on books dealing with ideas. Direct engagement was thereby *a priori* discarded'."[24] There are several ways to be indirect, though, and what is interesting about *Critique* is the extent to which Blanchot's reviews functioned as a model.

Blanchot was an enormous early influence on the journal. This influence is not merely a function of his role as an editor, nor is it due to the fact that he published many of his best essays throughout the early numbers, though both of these obviously played an important role. Blanchot's texts were taken as the very model of what a review should look like. In the proposal for the review which Bataille submitted to Maurice Giordias (whose idea it was to start the review), Bataille is quite explicit about this. In a section entitled "Character of the Reviews," which mostly discusses their length, we read, "We would like, for a model, to follow the studies of Maurice Blanchot (now published in *L'Arche* or collected in *Faux Pas*)."[25]

The consequence of this particular incarnation of the review-form was the institutionalization of a set of conventions which are in fundamental disaccord with those conventions of review and commentary currently operative in the Anglo-American world. When we pick up the *New York Review of Books*, for example, we expect an informed evaluation of the book under review by an "expert," not an act of creation which works by manipulating the processes of circulation and transmission.

Generalized buggery

Deleuze, we might say, makes two basic modifications to this review form. First, he expands it to the extent of the monograph. It's not that this had not been done—Klossowski's *Sade My Neighbor* was published in 1947, for example—but it was rare. Deleuze's monographs consistently and rigorously adopt the basic characteristics of the review form—most notably insofar as they adopt the position of a commentator only to create more effectively. In addition to this, and more importantly for our purposes here, Deleuze also generalized his approach. The review form required that one always spoke about another person—the author of the book under review. But Deleuze extends his ventriloquism to include not just other authors, but pretty much anything. It can be science, but also wolf packs, dance, cinema, plainchant, entire rat populations, musical forms, root structures, paintings, war, cartoons, and so on.

This indirection further disrupts our habits of reading and requires that we develop new techniques for making sense of Deleuze's texts.

This ventriloquism has obvious relations to my two previous propositions. In accordance with the first, there is no goodwill in Deleuze's historical commentaries. We can never expect Deleuze to efface himself from his commentary and try to present Nietzsche, for example, as clearly as possible. And this becomes even more apparent in its conformity with the second proposition—that because of the mobility of language we can never be certain about the meaning of words. One of the immediate consequences of Deleuze's ventriloquism is that certain words—and usually names—become unsettled: when Deleuze says, "Nietzsche says..." does the proper name actually refer to Nietzsche or to Deleuze? And in generalizing buggery to wolf packs and root structures, this ventriloquism does not bear only on proper names. When Deleuze writes "art" or "philosophy" or "science" in *What is Philosophy?*, does he really claim to speak about each of these, or is he using these words to work through the problems specific to his own system?

Thus to these first two propositions—Deleuze writes with a will to deceive and his words exploit the mobility of language—ventriloquism adds a third: Deleuze proceeds indirectly.

Perspectivism

In addition to being deceptive, initially meaningless, and consistently indirect, Deleuze's statements are always uttered from a specific point of view. While this is probably true of any statement, Deleuze is particularly conscious of it and exploits it to often spectacular effect. If we are not equally aware of this perspectivism, however, the effect is not spectacular but simply confusing.

Take, for example, these three statements from the second chapter of *Difference and Repetition* in which Deleuze develops his account of temporal synthesis.

1 The synthesis of time constitutes the present in time. It is not that the present is a dimension of time: the present alone exists. Rather, synthesis constitutes time as a living present, and the past and the future as dimensions of this present.[26]

2   The past, far from being a dimension of time, is the synthesis of all time of which the present and future are only dimensions.[27]

3   In this final synthesis of time, the present and past are in turn no more than dimensions of the future.[28]

The present is the totality of time. The past is the totality of time. The future is the totality of time. These three propositions do not contradict one another. But this is not because the first is a hypothesis which the second improved upon only to be supplanted finally by the truth of the third proposition. Each proposition is entirely true, but only by virtue of the point of view from which it is spoken. From the point of view of the first synthesis, the present alone exists. From the point of view of the second synthesis, the past alone exists. And from the point of view of the third synthesis, the future is the totality of time. This is a central aspect of Deleuze's style. He often installs himself in the position of the thing he wants to describe and describes the view from there. What does the first passive synthesis look like from the point of view of that synthesis? What does the world look like from the point of view of the larval subject?

This perspectivism raises a difficult question. Is there a stable set of coordinates across which the viewpoint changes? Are the positions which he adopts constrained by any kind of system? The initial answer seems to be that they are not, if only because Deleuze is not an obviously systematic thinker. The easy answer to this question would be to say that Deleuze's perspectives are determined by problems and that problems are the signs of certain encounters. But Deleuze himself was very attentive to the question of perspective in the authors he wrote about and taught, and his discussions of perspective in these authors is instructive here.

Take, as a first example, the variability of viewpoints Deleuze identifies for Spinoza's common notions. Deleuze writes that there are different "kinds of such notions. Spinoza says that common notions may be more or less useful, more or less easily formed and also more or less universal—that is they are organized in terms of greater or lesser generality of their viewpoints."[29] Here, common notions can be organized from three points of view: utility, formation, and generality. In addition to these variables, Deleuze adds a fourth: Spinoza's passages are subject to a *systemic* variability of perspective. Thus, discussing a particularly difficult passage in Spinoza, Deleuze explains that "if the passage raises many difficulties, this is because it is written from the viewpoint of the highest mode of perception or kind of knowledge."[30] In Deleuze's Spinoza, then, there are at least four coordinates along which one can change one's viewpoint: utility, genesis, generality, and systemic level.

Deleuze's discussion of Leibniz on this point is an even better example of both the importance perspective has for interpretation and the coordinates along which perspectives may or may not move.

Depending on Leibniz's correspondent or on the public to which he addressed himself, he presented his whole system at a particular level. Imagine that his system is made of levels more or less contracted or more or less relaxed; in order to explain something to someone, he goes to situate himself on a particular level of his system. Let us assume that the someone in question was suspected by Leibniz of having a mediocre intelligence: very well, he is delighted, he situates himself on one of the lowest levels of his system, and if he addresses someone of higher intelligence, he jumps to a higher level. As these levels belong implicitly to Leibniz's own texts, that creates a great problem for commentary. It's complicated because, in my opinion, one can never rely on a Leibniz text if one has not first discerned the system level to which this text corresponds. For example, there are texts in which Leibniz explains what, according to him, is the union of soul and body, right, and it's to one particular correspondent or another; to another correspondent, he will explain that there is no problem in the union of soul and body since the real problem is that of the relation of souls to one another. The two things are not at all contradictory, it's two levels of the system. The result is that if one does not evaluate the level of a Leibniz text, then one will get the impression that he constantly contradicts himself, when in fact, he does not contradict himself at all.[31]

To the four variables in Spinoza's texts we can add a fifth: the point of view of the interlocutor. One can adopt the point of view of one's correspondent. Already, then, we can see that the coordinates across which the point of view can move occupy multiple dimensions, and thus that mobility of perspectives is potentially infinite. But there is also a crucial constant across all the three of these examples—the syntheses of *Difference and Repetition*, *Expressionism and Philosophy*, and his Leibniz lecture—and that is the centrality of system. This is the main set of coordinates across which Deleuze's Spinoza and Leibniz move, and I will argue that this is even more true of Deleuze himself. Deleuze is always speaking from a determinate position within the philosophical system he elaborated across his texts.

This leads to a fourth habit that Deleuze requires us to take up: there is no view from nowhere; the truth of every utterance is positional, and, as readers, we need to discover the point of view from which the utterance is spoken. This raises the immediate question of how we are to locate an utterance or where we are supposed to locate it. And as I've just intimated, the answer is going to be that it must be located within Deleuze's system. But before I can make this point at all convincing, I have to turn toward the fifth characteristic of Deleuze's style: in addition to ill will, the rejection of convention, ventriloquism, and perspectivism, Deleuze's texts manifest a remarkable monotony.

Monotony

I began this chapter by quoting Deleuze's famous declaration that his texts on other authors were "monstrous" conceptual productions. Alain Badiou has flatly denied this. Far from being monstrous, Deleuze's texts are monotonous. Badiou explains that

> ... in starting from innumerable and seemingly disparate cases, in exposing himself to the impulsion organized by Spinoza and Sacher-Masoch, Carmelo Bene and Whitehead, Melville and Jean-Luc Godard, Francis Bacon and Nietzsche, Deleuze arrives at conceptual productions that I would unhesitatingly qualify as *monotonous*, composing a very particular regime of emphasis or almost infinite repetition of a limited repertoire of concepts, as well as a virtuosic variation of names, under which what is thought remains essentially identical.[32]

Badiou's description here characterizes our initial experience with Deleuze's texts. We are at first struck by the radical heterogeneity of concepts drawn, it would seem, from every corner of the contemporary world. However, it is impossible to ignore that across this heterogeneity there are certain concepts that continually reappear so that a family of rats, a pack of wolves, a rhizome, and the transcendental Idea all come to share the same essential predicates. And these patterns become the subsequent object of our attention—or, rather, (I will argue) they *should* become the object of our critical attention because this repetition of predicates across various incarnations suggests that there is a more stable concept, somewhere, animating Deleuze's "cases."

The possibility of this network of concepts which remains constant under the virtuosic variation of names leads to what we might call "a third kind of encounter" with Deleuze's texts or a third stage in our aesthetic education. In the first kind of encounter, Deleuze's texts are confusing and bewildering. We are all Lecercle's yuppie, furrowing our brows. But when we persist with the text, we start carving out certain spaces of meaning, most often—if the evolution of Deleuze studies is any indication—by following Deleuze's mostly implicit evaluations. Transcendence is bad; immanence is good. Reactivity is bad; activity is good. Trees are bad; rhizomes are good. The problem with this second kind of knowledge is that it is never clear why or from what point of view rhizomes, for example, are good and trees bad. There are a number of strategies for explaining why, but I think Badiou's observation puts us on the right track to answering these questions with any kind of authority insofar as it pushes us into a third kind of encounter with Deleuze's texts. To affirm Deleuze's monotony is to begin forming the idea of something common across Deleuze's texts by seeking out relations not on the basis of implicit valuations but according to the conceptual configurations which lie under Deleuze's variation of names.

Another way of putting this is to say that Deleuze's hidden emissions and slippages all tend toward the same basic underlying structure. Badiou captures at least two of the essential characteristics of this monotony: (1) a virtuosic variation of names, and (2) the essentially identical thought which underlies this variation. These two problems pose serious difficulties for any reading of Deleuze, and I will develop them below. But before defending Badiou's assertion, it is worth emphasizing that monotony and monstrosity by no means cancel one another out as he implies. Deleuze's texts are still capable of grandiose monstrosity, but precisely because of the requirements imposed by monotony.

Unproblematic monotony

The best way to demonstrate this monotony and to illustrate the particular difficulties it poses for reading Deleuze is by taking an easy and relatively unproblematic example from the second chapter of *Difference and Repetition*. In this chapter, Deleuze develops his account of the three passive syntheses. What makes this chapter illustrative of Deleuze's monotony is that there is not one account of passive synthesis, but three.

The first account is developed in the language of faculty psychology. A passive and spontaneous *imagination* contracts "agitations," "elements," or passing "instants" of time into one momentary but coherent "living present." But this lived present itself passes in the time. It, therefore, requires a second synthesis, this time operated by another faculty of the soul: *memory*. As the self's presents run off, they are conserved in this past, a pure past which has never been present. But now, the passive self has two representations before it—it walks with a limp on one green leg and one red leg, as Deleuze says—and it has to bring these two into some kind of relation by means of a third passive synthesis. This third synthesis is operated by yet a third faculty of the soul, *thought*. Sometimes, it succeeds in uniting the representations, but sometimes it fails.[33]

The second account unfolds in an entirely different technical vocabulary, that of psychoanalysis. Now, there is no spontaneous imagination synthesizing its agitations, but a series of "local egos" distributed across the "Id," a "field of individuation in which differences in intensity are distributed here and there."[34] These local egos "bind" the intensities scattered across the Id. This first passive synthesis along with its bound excitations is then extended in a second synthesis which gathers up and conserves these bound excitations[35] in a pure past.[36] But again, there are now two representations and, again, these are brought together in a third passive synthesis. There is a slight change of emphasis here, in that the third synthesis now propels the passive self onto another plane, but the operation is functionally the same in that this propulsion takes place by virtue of the attempt to bring the two prior syntheses under one.

Finally, the third account of passive synthesis makes use of yet a third technical vocabulary. Now, the first synthesis is a physical "coupling" of forces. This coupling is then extended into a resonance—a second synthesis—and this process ends with a third synthesis in which, again a "forced movement" launches the passive self out of itself and onto a new plane.[37]

Now, it is obvious that there is a functional similarity between each of these three accounts of synthesis. A passive self synthesizes its affections; these affections are retained in a passive memory; and the unity of apprehension and retention is accomplished in a third synthesis. But the point I want to make here is that the differences and repetitions across each account go without any explicit commentary on Deleuze's part.[38] There is absolutely no indication as to how we should read the translation of synthesis into drives and then into physical phenomena. And what's more, the only thing to indicate the difference between these three accounts is a section break in the analytic table of contents (this formatting of the table of contents has not been retained in any of the English translations). The distinction between these accounts of synthesis and their relation goes without comment. This is not entirely problematic. In fact, most commentators seem to think that it requires little to no comment. But, there are three important lessons with respect to Deleuze's style that we can derive from this short text.

The first is that we can see clearly the two characteristics of Deleuze's monotony that Badiou pointed out: there are certain sets of conceptual configurations which repeat themselves under a radical variation of names. In this case, the stable configuration is that of a progressive synthesis which begins with the earliest stages of the passive self and ends by pushing the passive self onto a new plane. The variation of names is clear in the movement from faculty psychology to psychoanalysis to physical systems.

The second is that one presentation does not seem to take precedence over another. Neither the theory of drives nor the physical theory of coupling seems to be the truth of the faculty psychology, for example. Conversely, Deleuze does not seem to be saying that in order to understand the relations between two pendulums we need to attribute to each pendulum an Id, an imagination and a memory. Rather, it seems that Deleuze is opening up a mobile conceptual space between all three of these accounts in which it is possible to think the abstract set of relations by which the passive self is temporally constituted without limiting thought to any particular formulation.

Third, this abstraction to a general conceptual configuration depends on some kind of textual limit. The relations and the conceptual mobility by which they are expressed are relatively easy to determine when everything is contained within the limits of one chapter of one text. In this case the space of substitution is well defined. But this example obviously is not what Badiou had in mind. The real question is what we do when we want to make these connections across texts. In this situation, monotony poses enormous interpretive difficulties, for we no longer have an external limit like a chapter.[39] When we move between two of Deleuze's texts, we have to find ways to spot the monotony by other means. And this leads us to the real problem of monotony.

Problematic monotony

When we leave the confines of a particular chapter or a particular book, we run into a whole series of difficulties, the central of which is that we no longer know what to align a certain conceptual configuration with. If the confines of the chapter stipulate that we're dealing with three passive syntheses, then we have no trouble coordinating them. This is far less easy with other texts.

Take, for example, *A Thousand Plateaus*' eleventh plateau: "1837: Of the Refrain (*ritournelle*)." It opens with three numbered paragraphs, the contents of which are in turn developed across the three parts of the main body of the text. The first paragraph begins with this scene:

> A child in the dark, gripped with fear, comforts himself by singing under his breath. He walks and halts to his song. Lost, he takes shelter, or orients himself with his little song as best he can.

The song is like a rough sketch of a calming and stabilizing, calm and stable center in the heart of chaos. Perhaps the child skips as he sings, hastens or slows his place. But the song itself is already a skip: it jumps from chaos to the beginnings of order in chaos and is in danger of breaking apart at any moment.[40]

In the scene of the second paragraph, we are suddenly at home. The little, fragile space of order marked out by the song in the first scene is now considerably stronger: the structure of the house keeps the forces of chaos at bay through an activity of selection, elimination, and extraction. Through these operations, the "germinal forces" of the child's song are secured so that they might be directed toward other tasks, like homework.[41]

Finally, in the third scene this world, closed off from chaos, begins to crack and open on to an outside—"not on the side where the old forces of chaos press against it but in another region, one created by the circle itself."[42] This crack provides an opening through which the child can "launch forth" into a strange cosmic order join with the "forces of the future."[43]

It seems obvious that Deleuze and Guattari are not making a statement about little songs as such or about the virtues of singing in uncomfortable situations. But it is not immediately clear what point they are making instead. A traditional answer has been to say that they are talking about "territorialization" understood in a general sense ranging from that set of processes by which a new apartment begins to feel like home to the institution of geopolitical boundaries. This makes immediate sense. To justify this reading we first coordinate these three scenes with the discussion of territorialization later in the chapter and then compare the two concepts: territory and child carving out a space of familiarity through song. We can then link this text with Deleuze's others by virtue of the concept of territorialization: to the logical discussion of territory in *Difference and Repetition*, and to the political discussion in *Anti-Oedipus*, we can add this aesthetic discussion.

This reading, while initially persuasive, forces us to overlook much of what is going on in the passage, however. If the generality of the concept of territory employed here has the virtue of letting us take the scene more or less literally, it also forces us to abandon all sorts of other things: why do we move from chaos to home to *cosmos*? Why does it matter that this movement to the cosmos is not made by venturing back into chaos but into another region determined by the circle itself? Why does each scene have a different temporality? Not only does this reading force us to abandon much of the detail of the text, it establishes the relationship between texts on the basis of one word: in this instance, territory. I think a way out of this dilemma, and one which will allow us to coordinate these conceptual configurations with more rigor, is to abandon the virtues of a literal reading and emphasize the final two characteristics of Deleuze's style that I will develop here: Deleuze's heavy reliance on metaphor and his rigorous functionalism.

Kill metaphor

To say that Deleuze is a deeply figurative writer runs into the immediate problem of his apparent animosity toward metaphor. Monotony instantly metaphorizes everything, but Deleuze repeatedly insisted across his oeuvre and in interviews that he was not using metaphors. He said on multiple occasions that his engagement with scientific and mathematical models was just that: an engagement with models, not metaphor. This position is most developed in Deleuze and Guattari's *Kafka*. Over the course of the text, they develop a coordinated set of arguments against metaphor.

Their general position (and its difficulties) is best captured in the short imperative, "Kill metaphor."[44] The problem with such an imperative, of course, is that it is itself a metaphor insofar as metaphor becomes something susceptible to murder. The problems continue if we notice that this imperative is enjoined by a determinate end: "hyper-realism."[45] We kill metaphor in the name of a rigorous literalism. But this works equally poorly as a description of both Deleuze's and Kafka's prose. If we insist on a hyper-realism characterized by a hyper-literalness, we lose any ability to make sense of some of Deleuze's best sentences: "[N]ever is a plateau separable from the cows that populate it, which are also clouds in the sky."[46] Or: "Be the Pink Panther and your loves will be like the wasp and the orchid, the cat and the baboon."[47] Or: "The power of the false is delicate, allowing itself to be recaptured by frogs and scorpions."[48] We are put in the uncomfortable position of trying to explain how Nietzsche, quite literally, took Deleuze from behind.

In *Kafka*, Deleuze and Guattari reject metaphor (on the basis of a short passage from Kafka's *Diaries*) for two additional reasons. The first is that it allows them to develop their concept of becoming-animal. The appearance of investigative dogs and singing mice in Kafka's stories has nothing metaphorical about it, Deleuze and Guattari argue. Rather, Kafka reveals in this way our essential complicity with our bodies, "the animal or the meat."[49] In this sense, the rejection of metaphor is specific to *Kafka*, and we cannot generalize it to Deleuze's other works. The other reason they reject metaphor is that it is too easily understood as mere ornament or figuration, and this refusal to reject an understanding of metaphor as an "arbitrary"[50] comparison, I think, we *can* generalize. What they are interested in is the real work of transfer a metaphor accomplishes, the way in which it performs a real distribution across a field of intensity. As Deleuze (or Parnet) puts it in *Dialogues*, "It is never a matter of metaphor; there are no metaphors, only combinations."[51] The problem, then, with the concept of metaphor is that it allows us to too quickly dismiss a figure as a mere ornament without acknowledging the real distribution a metaphor accomplishes.[52]

The problem with this argument for Deleuze's readers, however, is that the combination that a metaphor performs does not result in an absolute identity of the two terms. There is a transfer of *some* characteristics from one term to another, and as a result, in the transfer, some predicates are retained and some left behind. Thus, even if we say there are no metaphors but only real combinations (in theory), we are still faced with the practical need to make an interpretive decision and thus the whole problem of metaphor reappears. When we imagine the little whistling child in the ritornello, which aspects of these three scenes do we keep and which do we abandon? I will propose an answer to this question below, but my argument here is that while Deleuze's monotony tends to metaphorize everything insofar as it uproots most statements from their literal meanings, far from posing the false problem of metaphor (does Deleuze use metaphors or not?), monotony actually solves the real problem (which predicates do we retain and which do we abandon?), in that it provides us with a rigorous way of selecting which predicates to retain and which to leave behind.

Functions

The main difficulty posed by Deleuze's monotony as I have presented it thus far is simply that when we wish to move between texts, there is no external limit to guide us. There is a further problem that I have not yet mentioned, and it is the extent of Deleuze's virtuosity in varying names (and this, of course, is closely related to the second characteristic of Deleuze's style described above: the signification of words is not constant in Deleuze). The central problem is that this virtuosic variation of names does not leave Deleuze's central concepts untouched. Take, for example, the "plane of immanence." What he calls the "plane of immanence" in *Cinema I* is what he calls the "plane of composition" in *What is Philosophy?*. The plane of immanence is still present in *What is Philosophy?*, but it now functions in the same way that the "time-image" did in *Cinema II*. There is an exact inversion of names between the two books. The same thing happens with the opposition of intensity and extensity between *Expressionism in Philosophy* and *Difference and Repetition*, both texts published in 1969. What he calls "extensive parts" in *Expressionism*, he calls "intensity" in *Difference and Repetition*. This variability applies to a whole list of Deleuze's central concepts: multiplicity, singularity, art, virtuality, assemblage, territorialization, deterritorialization, differential relation. Each of these terms undergoes substantial reversals of meaning across Deleuze's texts. Any attempt to understand what Deleuze means by "multiplicity" or "singularity" which proceeds by amassing sentences which have those words in them and which pretend to speak about them, then, risks radically missing the point.

As Badiou pointed out and as I have briefly shown, there is under this virtuosic catachresis a monotonous conceptual structure, and it is precisely because of the persistence of this structure that we can know that these concepts change their sense. What Deleuze calls "multiplicity" or "singularity" in *Anti-Oedipus* refers to a completely different moment of this monotony that it does in *Difference and*

Repetition,⁵³ for example, because across different texts, they refer to different places in one monotonous structure. The immediate consequence of this variability is that *we cannot make connections across texts on the basis of a linguistic identity*. The identity has to be structural. Deleuze himself spoke rather directly about this in another lecture on Leibniz.

> Concepts in philosophy are not a single word. A great philosophical concept is a complex, a proposition, or a prepositional *function*. One would have to do exercises in philosophical grammar. Philosophical grammar would consist of this: with a given concept, find the verb. If you have not found the verb, if you have not rendered the verb dynamic, you cannot live it. . . . What is the verb? Sometimes the philosopher states it explicitly, sometimes he does not state it.

Deleuze does not limit this way of reading to Leibniz. An excellent example of this is Deleuze's own reading of Spinoza which takes the concept of expression as its focal point. As Pierre Macherey notes, "The noun *expressio* does not once occur, and the idea of expression is suggested only through the use of the verb *expimere* which occurs in various forms . . . altogether forty-six times."⁵⁴ Macherey implies that this weakens the strength of Deleuze's emphasis, but it arguably strengthens it insofar as the emphasis falls on the verb and not its attendant concepts. For Deleuze, it is the verb which pulls the system together and expresses its complex movement.

In any case, I would argue that this is the question we need to ask in order to get away from our subjection to the names of concepts and to the play of adjectives: what is the verb? This approach to reading is very clearly based on Deleuze's "functionalism": do not ask what a concept means; ask what it does, but it operates at the level of the molar as well. The question we need to ask is not "which nouns share the same predicates," but "how, and, in relation to what other concepts does a certain concept function"?

One of the great advantages of emphasizing function is that it foregrounds the dynamism of Deleuze's concepts. "Monotony" suggests a kind of abstract and static set of relationships between concepts and implies that Deleuze simply got caught in an intellectual rut. But the space in which Deleuze's thought unfolds is not marked by stasis, despite the monotony of concepts. It is marked, rather, by an extreme mobility. This is, Bergson claimed, what "characterizes the signs of human language." It "is not so much their generality as their mobility."[55] And Deleuze takes full advantage of this characteristic to create concepts which are genuinely genetic. Functionalism assumes a dynamic relationship between concepts, and it thus allows us to understand this system in relation to one of Deleuze's central concerns: genesis. Each moment of Deleuze's system engenders the next and thus all of his central concepts are in a series of complex and mobile relationships with one another. Their function, then, is not related to what they can do in the world, but what they do in relation to one another.

We can apply this thesis to the concepts of the ritornello. Notice, now, the play of functions in the three scenes of the ritornello. The child, by humming a song, organizes chaos into a fragile order. In the second scene, the order secured in the first scene is considerably strengthened by the house. In the third scene, the order is so secure that the child can launch forth with confidence into new territories. We thus get a picture of the gradual genesis of order out of chaos.

Notice, too, that there is a definite temporal aspect to each stage. The first moment clearly marks out a space in the present. The second stage selects, filters, and thus *retains* certain elements of the chaos. The third opens the child onto a cosmic plane on which it joins the forces of the future. At each moment, then, the song, by virtue of its rhythm, carves out a temporal space, a living present, a space of retention, and a space of a future. All of this should recall the doctrine of passive synthesis I presented earlier in the chapter.

This functional equivalence is what guides our reading of the metaphor of the child as well. The first thing it tells us is that as we move from a metaphorical to a philosophical reading, we need to abandon all the anthropomorphisms which indicate a well-constituted world. This particular conceptual configuration, in the rest of Deleuze's work, does not apply to a well-developed child, capable of getting lost, whistling and doing homework. In the *Logic of Sense*, it refers to infants capable of eating, vomiting, and excretion. In *Difference and Repetition*, it refers to a *passive* and spontaneous imagination. What we retain, then, is the idea of an initial rhythm—that of the song—going through a series of modifications (the three passive syntheses) by which it eventually creates order and gives the passive self a kind of autonomy which will function as the ground of its activity. This is still a process of territorialization, as most readings would have it, but it is far more specific: it is by means of the three syntheses that the subject gives order to its world and liberates itself from its passive affections. What I want to emphasize here, however, is that these interpretive decisions are made through a functional coordination of concepts across texts.

Aesthetic education

Badiou's problem is perhaps *the* central problem of reading Deleuze. Manuel DeLanda, one of the few commentators to have noticed this play of concept and name, puts the problem this way: "Gilles Deleuze changes his terminology in every one of his books. Very few of his concepts retain their names or linguistic identity."[56] Condensed in this statement are the two problems Badiou noted. First is the problem of Deleuze's frequent changes in terminology. His concepts do not retain a consistent and reliable "linguistic identity." In a very direct sense, then, we cannot agree, as friends would, on the signification of words. The implication of this, however, is that while the names of the concepts change across books, the concepts themselves remain relatively stable. This is the second problem: underneath the shifting variations in names, Deleuze's concepts remain stable; while they forego their linguistic identity, they retain a conceptual identity.

In a sense, this characteristic of Deleuze's style incorporates and makes use of all of the former ones: it requires an initial deception; it performs a destabilization of linguistic identity or the agreed-upon relations between words and things; it functions by means of a generalized indirection; it provides the coordinates for the variations in perspective; and finally, it is metaphorical, or even allegorical. But it also provides a way of navigating the difficulties raised by these stylistic devices and the immense difficulties posed by Deleuze's texts. By focusing on functional relationships and the migration of these functional relationships across Deleuze's *oeuvre*, we can construct significantly more coherent readings of his work. This is the approach I took in *Deleuze and the Genesis of Representation*, and it is the approach I will use throughout the rest of this book.

One final question I want to begin to address—one which continually arises whenever we talk about Deleuze's style and which I only provided incidental and passing answers to above—is *why?* Why make all of these moves and do all of these things which can only manifest themselves as annoyances and as basic affronts to the demands of instant legibility which we have learned to expect from expository prose? There are a number of answers to this question, most of which are grounded in Deleuze's basic philosophical concepts: the disruption of habit, the opening up of a mobile space of "sense" in which we make connections and form constellations which then bring meaning back to the text, and a number of others I have not touched upon here.

One of the most important reasons we might give for these stylistic maneuvers is that for Deleuze, philosophy has a strong aesthetic dimension. It is manifestly not the attempt to speak the truth as clearly, directly, and blandly as possible; the ideal is not a language without recourse to detour or distraction and in which all characters populating examples are named Smith. In *Difference and Repetition*, one of Deleuze's most interesting criticisms of Hegel is played out not at the level of Hegel's concepts, but at the level of the invention of concepts and the ways in which Hegel invented his concepts. Hegel, Deleuze contends, merely tried to represent the movement of thought.

> It is not enough . . . to propose a new representation of movement; representation is already mediation. Rather, it is a question of producing within the work a movement capable of affecting the mind outside of all representation; it is a question of making movement itself a work, without interposition; of substituting direct signs for mediate representations; of inventing vibrations, rotations, whirlings, gravitations, dances or leaps which directly touch the mind.[57]

Deleuze and Hegel both work through a similar problem: what is the movement of thought. But Hegel tried to *represent* the movement of thought and *this* led to overly broad concepts. Instead, one must become the Nietzschean philosopher-artist and try to write in such a way that the reader's mind is *directly* affected by the work, not at the level of representation and its concepts but at the much more chaotic and unstable level of the text's moving signs. Deleuze is not content to tell us about his new image of thought. He wants us to live it.

It is equally the case, however, that we cannot remain at the level of vibrations and rotations, and that as reading progresses, we move from these whirlings of the purely intensive text through implicit valuations and ultimately to the idea of something common between texts. This is the point at which this book intervenes. It is an attempt to think in the space of mobility opened up Deleuze's style and to articulate what is common to Deleuze's texts. Its main goal is to aid in the creation of an abstract and monotonous conceptual configuration. As I will argue over the next three chapters, that conceptual configuration looks basically like this:

1. Unindividuated matter
2. First passive synthesis
3. Second passive synthesis
4. Third passive synthesis
5. Transcendental Field
6. First active synthesis (Good sense)
7. Second active synthesis (Common sense)
8. Representation/Individuals

2

Ontology

The force which is evolving throughout the organized world is a limited force, which is always seeking to transcend itself and always remains inadequate to the work it would fain produce.[1]

The beginning is truly in the void; it is suspended in the void. It is with-out.[2]

This eight-part structure, toward which Deleuze's "hidden emissions" and "slippages" all tend, is at the foundation of his ontology. Deleuze's ontology is usually approached negatively. We know, for example, that he is not Plato, that he is for immanence rather than transcendence, the multiple rather than the one, difference rather than identity, rhizomes rather than trees, and so on. But these approaches tend to miss is the central problem animating Deleuze's thought. That problem, Christian Kerslake has persuasively argued, is the completion of the Kantian project: "Deleuze represents the latest flowering of the project, begun in the immediate wake of Kant's *Critique of Pure Reason*, to complete consistently the 'Copernican revolution' in philosophy."[3] Deleuze himself regularly asserted as much. In *What is Grounding?* (1956), a seminal lecture which laid much of the foundation for *Difference and Repetition*, he had already described his project as a taking up of the "Kantian enterprise." This was also the explicit project, I will argue below, of *Nietzsche and Philosophy* (1962). At the heart of *Difference and Repetition* (1968), Deleuze again characterized his project as one of taking up the "Kantian initiative" and carrying it to completion.[4] Even those texts which do not explicitly claim to complete the Kantian enterprise are very obviously concerned with it. Deleuze's Hume, for example, consistently returns to and develops major Kantian themes. His Proust is concerned with developing a Kantian doctrine of the faculties.[5] Deleuze's Spinoza moves toward a Kantian theory of ideas and even a latent schematism.[6] This raises the question, then, of what Deleuze means by the "Kantian initiative." What does it mean to complete consistently the Copernican revolution in philosophy?

The best way of approaching what it means to "take up the Kantian initiative" is to begin with what it does not mean. In his 1980 lectures on Leibniz, Deleuze borrowed Merleau-Ponty's characterization of the "classical" philosophers[7]:

> There is an author who said quite well what creates the family resemblance of philosophers of the 17th century, it was Merleau-Ponty. He wrote a small text on so-called classical philosophers of the seventeenth century, and he tried to characterize them in a lively way, and said that what is so incredible in these philosophers is an innocent way of thinking starting from and as a function of the infinite. That's what the classical century is.[8]

One month later, in another lecture, Deleuze repeated this formulation, and slightly developed the claim:

> In all cases, the point [the classical philosophers] start from is infinity. Philosophers have an innocent way of thinking starting from infinity, and they give themselves to infinity. There was infinity everywhere, in God and in the world. That let them undertake things like infinitesimal analysis. An innocent way of thinking starting from infinity means a world of creation.[9]

This innocent way of starting from infinity, Deleuze says in *Expressionism in Philosophy*, is the "secret of grand Rationalism" of which Spinoza is "the most perfect embodiment."[10] And perhaps because Deleuze calls Spinoza the "prince" of philosophers[11] or the

"Christ of philosophers,"[12] several of Deleuze's readers have attributed this act of innocence to Deleuze himself.[13] Nothing could be further from the case, however. Classical philosophers start innocently from the concept of infinity; Deleuze is well aware that after Kant this is no longer possible.

When Deleuze describes Kant's Copernican revolution, he does it in more or less traditional terms. The classical philosophers begin with the idea of an infinite web of subjects and objects united in a pre-established harmony, but Kant "proposes" the idea of a "necessary submission of the object to the 'finite' subject: to us, the legislators, in our very finitude" (KCP 69). As Kant famously put it in the introduction to the first Critique, "Up to now it has been assumed that all our cognition must conform to the objects." What happens, Kant asks, if we assume instead that "the objects must conform to our cognition"?[14] The first thing that happens is that we no longer begin with an infinity to which we strive to become adequate. Instead, we begin with the concept of finitude. Our relationship with objects is no longer settled in advance by a pre-established harmony. Objects are subject to *our* legislative understanding, and we know them according to the basic forms of our understanding (the categories). From now on, everything is referred to the subject. It is us, finite individuals, Deleuze says, who are "giving the orders" (KCP 14).

It is for this reason that Deleuze, immediately following his claim that "An innocent way of thinking starting from infinity means a world of creation," adds this: "They [the classical philosophers] could go quite far, but not all the way."[15] What the innocence of the classical philosophers prevented them from seeing was subjectivity defined as constitutive finitude.

The finite ego is the true founding. Thus the first principle becomes finitude. For the Classics, finitude is a consequence, the limitation of something infinite. The created world is finite, the Classics tell us, because it is limited. The finite ego founds the world and knowledge of the world because the finite ego is itself the constitutive founding of what appears. In other words, it is finitude that is the founding of the world. The relations of the infinite to the finite shift completely. The finite will no longer be a limitation of the infinite; rather, the infinite will be an overcoming [dépassement] of the finite. Moreover, it is a property of the finite to surpass and go beyond itself. The notion of self-overcoming [auto-dépassement] begins to be developed in philosophy. It will traverse all of Hegel and will reach into Nietzsche. The infinite is no longer separable from an act of overcoming finitude because only finitude can overcome itself.[16]

This is a clunky passage, but it makes several important points, some of which I will return to below. The most general point it makes is simply that (after Kant) we can no longer begin innocently in the infinite. We need to make an essential detour through the subject understood as a finite ego. It's not that the classical philosophers did not have a concept of subjectivity—Descartes' *cogito* still remains a central model of subjectivity, for example—it's that they could not think subjectivity, or "the finite ego itself," as constitutive "of the world and of knowledge of the world." They could not conceive of it as "the constitutive founding of what appears." This, Deleuze said twenty-four years earlier in *What is Grounding?* (1956), was the great discovery of Kant: the discovery of our "*constitutive finitude.*"[17]

Thus the first among many ways of understanding what it means to "take up the Kantian enterprise" and carry it to its fulfillment, then, is that we have to take an essential detour through the subject. If the ultimate goal of metaphysics is still to establish a speculative relation, this can only happen by following, as Meillassoux puts it, the "narrow passage" to the "great outdoors."[18] For Deleuze, this narrow passage is that of constitutive finitude. Much of this chapter is concerned with describing the "finite ego" at the heart of Deleuze's thought and the process by which it "overcomes" itself.

It is perhaps worth addressing an immediate objection to this characterization of Deleuze's thought at the start. Is it not the case that Deleuze is the thinker of the impersonal and the pre-individual? Does he not consistently emphasize that whatever subjectivity we have is the consequence of our encounters with all sorts of nonhuman actors? And to make matters worse, Deleuze rarely uses the word "subject" after his first book. There are several ways of responding to these objections, many of which I hope will become clear over the next few chapters. One particularly important passage in *What is Grounding?* speaks directly to these questions, though, and it is worth quoting in full because it has so rarely been quoted.

> Hume brought along something new: the analysis of the structure of subjectivity. The word 'subject', as it happens, is very rarely used by Hume. This is not by chance. Hegel too analyzes subjectivity without pronouncing the word 'subject'. And Heidegger goes much further and says that the word 'subject' must not be used. Instead, it is necessary to designate it by the essential structure one discovers. If one gives an adequate definition of the subject, then one has no more reason to speak explicitly of it. Heidegger and Hegel both tell us that the subject is nothing other than a self-development. Hegel analyzes this dialectically: self-developing as self-transformation, with mediation as the essential process. Heidegger says that the essence of subjectivity is transcendence, but with a new sense: where previously this term was used to refer to the state of something transcendent, with Heidegger, it becomes the movement of self-transcendence. It is the mode of being of the movement that transcends (*le mouvement à ce qui se transcende*).[19]

Perhaps this passage goes too far in the other direction, in that it seems to suggest that there never was any other question than that of subjectivity. It does, however, outline what Deleuze, in 1956, imagined to be at stake in the fundamental questions of ontology after Kant. At the center of this passage is the problem of the articulation of a structure of subjectivity. The central task is to "designate the essential structure one discovers." But we might notice, too, that this structure is characterized as a movement of self-transcendence, or as he said in the 1980 lecture quoted above, of self-overcoming (*auto-dépassement*). This emphasis on the movement of subjectivity points us to one of Deleuze's central criticism of Kant, and thus to one of the central difficulties of taking up the Kantian initiative.

Synthesis

Before Deleuze takes his detour through subjectivity, he substantially revises the Kantian concepts which lead up to it. What we need, he writes in *Nietzsche and Philosophy*, is "a radical transformation of

Kantianism, a reinvention of the critique which Kant betrayed at the same time as he conceived it, a resumption of the critical project on a new basis and with new concepts."[20] Of all the concepts that need to be reinvented, the most important—and the one at the center of Kant's self-betrayal—is the concept of synthesis. "Kantianism centers on the concept of synthesis which it discovered," Deleuze writes, but Kant "endangered this discovery."[21]

Deleuze emphasizes two ways in which Kant endangered the concept of synthesis. One of them appears in the third chapter of *Difference and Repetition*. There Deleuze claimed that Kant reserved the powers of synthesis for the active self only. As a consequence, the "passive self is defined only by receptivity and, as such, endowed with no power of synthesis."[22] Indeed, between the two editions of the first *Critique*, Kant radically revised his conception of synthesis so that it was no longer the imagination ("a *blind* though indispensible" faculty) which gathered representations together, but the understanding, or the seat of our spontaneity, which carried out the act of synthesis.[23] Deleuze, following Husserl, goes back to the first edition of the *Critique* where the imagination blindly gathers together representations. He thus claims in *Difference and Repetition* that while "the Kantian initiative can be taken up," this can only happen on the condition of a "quite different understanding of the passive self."[24] We have to attribute to passivity a power of synthesis.

This is exactly what Deleuze himself had done in the second chapter of *Difference and Repetition*. He argued that the passive self is not an empty receptivity, but a series of passive *syntheses*—and further, that our receptivity or our "capacity for experiencing affections" was dependent on understanding these syntheses as *passive*.[25] The concept of passive synthesis has a long history but we can say in general that a synthesis can be passive in two senses. It can be passive first of all in the sense that we are not consciously aware of its work. To use an example from Merleau-Ponty's *Phenomenology of Perception*, if I hold a pencil in front of my eyes and stare past it, it will appear as two pencils. I know, "intellectually" that it is one, but passively it appears as two. If I shift my focus to the pencil itself, the two images become one without any intellectual effort on my part. It just happens, and the process by which it happens eludes conscious thought.[26] It is thus a passive synthesis.

A synthesis can also be passive in the sense that it is not subject to any rules. In Kant, for example, the categories—and indeed, concepts in general—function as rules for synthesis. They regulate the combination of representations. From this point of view, a passive synthesis is one which is preconceptual and does not have recourse to concepts. Deleuze's passive syntheses are passive in both senses. They are passive in the first sense insofar as they take place "in the mind," but are not carried out "by the mind."[27] But they are also preconceptual. There is no law regulating them.

This introduction of a doctrine of passive synthesis is the first way Deleuze claims to rescue Kant's discovery. But what is at stake in this question of passive synthesis is the possibility of thinking subjectivity from the point of view of its genesis.[28] This is Deleuze's second major revision of the Kantian notion of synthesis, and it is related to one of Deleuze's most persistent criticisms of Kant— namely, that while he invented concepts which were adequate to thinking about *possible* experience, Kant lacked the resources to think about the genesis of *real* experience. The strongest formulation of this complaint is in *Kant's Critical Philosophy*. There Deleuze explains that for Kant,

> the understanding legislates over phenomena, but only insofar as they are considered in the *form* of their intuition; its legislative acts (categories) therefore constitute *general* laws, and are exercised on nature as object of *possible* experience (every event has a cause...etc.). But understanding never determines *a priori* the *content* of phenomena, the detail of *real* experience or the *particular* laws of this or that object. These are known only empirically, and remain contingent in relation to our understanding.[29]

Kant (and for good reason) only grasped subjectivity as an empty form. Sensibility is the empty form of space and time. The understanding circulates through the pure formal relations of the categories. The imagination crosses the distance of these two faculties only by producing pure relations. One of the central tasks of Deleuze's philosophy, I will argue below, is to think through the *content* of phenomena and the *detail* of real experience. Instead of enumerating the general laws of possible objects (categories), he develops a theory of the particular laws of singular objects (Ideas). This project begins, however, with a reformulation of the very principle of synthesis. Throughout *Nietzsche and Philosophy*, Deleuze consistently reaffirms the necessity of inventing a new principle of synthesis. This new principle would have to have two characteristics. The first is that it would need to be a plastic principle. This is because the synthesis which follows from it will not be a synthesis of empty and static forms as the Kantian syntheses were. It will be a synthesis which takes root in the detail of real experience. To renew the Kantian enterprise, we need "an essentially *plastic* principle that is no wider than what it conditions, that changes itself with the conditioned and determines itself in each case along with what it determines."[30] It "is never separable from" from what it synthesizes.[31] As Deleuze puts it in *Difference and Repetition* (alluding to Plotinus), "the eye binds light; it is itself a bound light."[32] But this implies that the synthesizing subject is not yet separate from the conditions of its emergence. The subject, before it synthesizes, is part of the flux of unindividuated matter. This points to the second characteristic of this new principle. If the agent of synthesis is inseparable from the flux of matter, the principle which governs synthesis will also have to be "truly genetic and productive."[33] It will have to account for the possibility of a subjectivity which will emerge from life.

In a way, this is a further turn in the Copernican revolution. If the Kantian revolution was to make us legislators by submitting the object to our understanding, the Deleuzian revolution undoes this relation of submission. Deleuze's vision of thought is not that of a thought which "measures, limits and moulds life,"[34] but one which is the "affirmative power *of* life"—a kind of thought which thinks with life or even as life.[35] This further turn does not put us back in the territory of the classical philosophers, however. We do not set out again with or from a concept of infinity, but remain firmly within the perspective of a constitutive finitude.

Architecture

Despite these criticisms of Kant, Deleuze's central works still retain the basic architecture of Kant's first critique. This is most obvious in *Difference and Repetition*. We still have three syntheses; we still have a theory of Ideas; and we still have a schematism whereby concepts or Ideas are "*applied*" to sensibility (more about this below). All three of these conceptual groups undergo significant revisions in Deleuze's hands, of course. The syntheses are rethought as explicitly temporal and as emergent from a material flux; Deleuze's theory of Ideas radically revises the notion of Ideas in their structure (differential), nature (virtual), and extension (they apply to singular objects, not all objects); the Kantian schematism becomes dramatization; and, above all, Deleuze thinks about all of these concepts genetically, that is to say, within the context of their complex and functional relationships with one another. They emerge not from the empty forms of space and time but from the flux of life. But even with all of these modifications, we can still recognize the Kantian architecture.

The simplest way of making this point, although it involves another round of radical simplifications, is to follow Deleuze's introductory characterization of Kant in his lectures and in *Kant's Critical Philosophy*.[36] There are two movements or adventures in Kant, Deleuze says, and they go in opposite directions in relation to two faculties, sensibility and the understanding. The first adventure goes from spatiotemporal manifolds of sensibility to the concepts of the understanding. This movement proceeds by means of three syntheses—the synthesis of apprehension (which gathers together the manifold); the synthesis of reproduction (which records and reproduces the manifold) and the synthesis of recognition (which brings the manifold under a concept). The second movement, the schematism, goes in the opposite direction—from the understanding back to sensibility. Here, the imagination produces a "schema" which gives concepts spatiotemporal coordinates and thus makes their reentry into the space and time of sensibility possible.

Deleuze retains both of these movements in his own work. In *The Logic of Sense* he calls the first adventure the "dynamic genesis." It comprises three passive syntheses which move us from sensibility to the faculty of thought. He calls the second adventure the "static genesis." This genesis moves us from the Ideas of thought back to the "state of affairs" through a process of actualization or individuation. In the remainder of this chapter, I want to trace the way Deleuze replays both of these movements across his *oeuvre*.

The dynamic genesis

In the last chapter, I argued that the only way to get to the heart of Deleuze's project was to give up the search for key lines and disconnected passages and try instead to designate the underlying, monotonous structure. This structure characterizes a genesis or a process of self-transcendence, and this means among many things that each moment has to be understood in its functional relations to other moments of the structure. But because this structure is monotonous—that is to say, because it repeats itself in each of Deleuze's major texts—there is a proliferation of terms for each moment. I have tried to cover as many of these proliferations as possible. While I have tried to make what follows readable, it is still not easy going. I apologize in advance for this, and urge those readers who find it intolerable to look again at the chart at the end of the last chapter and then to skip ahead to the next two chapters where I describe this process as it unfolds in individual texts.

The original position

In *Cinema 1*, Deleuze begins his exposition of Bergson's thought by claiming that Bergson asks for two things and two things only: (1) a plane of immanence, understood as a field of unindividuated matter in a state of constant flux or movement and (2) an interval in that flux.[37] From this, the whole of Bergsonism can be "deduced."

This pair of concepts is also all that Deleuze himself ever asks for. His Hume can be deduced from a principle of difference (the ceaseless variation of circumstantial matter) and a principle of repetition (the habitual relations we establish in that matter) (ES 22–3). In *Nietzsche and Philosophy*, we need a "web of forces" and the principle of synthesis which relates those forces (the will to power) (NP 54). In *Difference and Repetition*, we need a flow of intensity and the synthesis which connects or binds these intensities (DR 70). In *The Logic of Sense* and *Anti-Oedipus*, we begin with flows of "partial objects" (the molecules of the molecular unconscious (AO 309, 323)), and the principle of synthesis which gathers together this multiplicity (the body without organs). These are the two givens of

Deleuze's system: a plane of unindividuated matter and a principle of synthesis. The first of these givens, the plane of unindividuated matter, is what Deleuze calls the "plane of immanence" in *Cinema 1* (though In *What is Philosophy?*, alluding to *Expressionism in Philosophy*, he calls it a "plane of composition"[38]. In *Difference and Repetition*, he calls it the "intensive field." His characterization of this field changes. In some texts, Deleuze suggests that this plane is characterized by the communication of extensive parts to infinity, and that the relations between parts are determined by the natural laws of movement and rest (EP, C1). When he makes these claims, however, it is always in the context of other philosophers who explicitly hold this position (or some variant of it)—namely, Spinoza and Bergson. When he speaks in something like his own name, the characterization changes. In both *Difference and Repetition* and *What is Philosophy?*, for example, this field is characterized by evanescence and discontinuity. In *Anti-Oedipus*, the partial objects scattered across this field are not related by the laws of movement and rest; rather, the only relation between them is the absence of a relation (AO 309). Most often, Deleuze simply characterizes this plane as chaotic, tumultuous and in constant flux and leaves it at that.

This is because, I would argue, he is most often thinking this material plane phenomenologically, or from the point of view of the larval subjects which inhabit it, and not from the God's-eye point of view adopted by the classical philosophers. From this point of view, the matter scattered across the plane of immanence is the matter of sensation. In *Anti-Oedipus*, for example, Deleuze and Guattari will say that it a "hyletic flux" (AO 36, 46) or that it is composed of "singularities" (AO 324) (it is worth saying that they are not using "singularity" in the mathematical sense operative in *Difference and Repetition*, but in the philosophical sense of the immediate objects of intuition). Similarly, in *Difference and Repetition*, Deleuze often uses the word "intensity" to characterize this field. And again, he is not using it in an exclusively scientific sense. Rather, he merges the concept of intensity with the Freudian sense of "excitations" which designate a tension caused by the intrusion of another body on mine (DR 96, 118). In *Nietzsche and Philosophy* and *Francis Bacon*, he describes this material field in the language of "forces" which affect my body and which my body reacts to (NP 62).³⁹ The material field from this point of view is a field of sensation experienced at the lowest level of our bodies—that level at which, as Bergson puts it, "we directly feel the flux" (MM 139).

This perspective carries us over to the second of Deleuze's givens: the "interval," the "power of synthesis," or the "larval subject" which gathers together passing instants of the material flux. Sometimes, Deleuze characterizes this subject physiologically as the "brain" (C1 62, WP 215) or "the nervous system" (FB 34, 52). Sometimes, he defines it psychologically as a spontaneous or passive imagination (DR, EP). Most often, he characterizes it metaphysically as a "body without organs" (AO, LS), or simply as "power" (EP, SPP). This latter characterization is the most precise in that it designates the central function of the passive self: its basic characteristic is that it is a "power of synthesis" (DI 21) or a "principle of synthesis" (NP 52). As Deleuze puts it in *The Logic of Sense*, it is a "liquid principle" which melts together the whirling parts of the material field (LS 90).

From the interaction of these two concepts—the material field and the fluid principle which inhabits it—Deleuze's entire system unfolds in the form a series of progressive syntheses. There are three passive syntheses, an ideal synthesis, and two active syntheses.

Passive synthesis

There are three passive syntheses, and together they form the system of the passive self (DR) or the "machinic unconscious" (AO 109). Deleuze gives the first passive synthesis a number of different names: habit (DR 73), imagination (DR 71, EP 241), connective synthesis (AO, LS), vibration (WP 168; FB 72), and perception (C1 62) to name only the most prominent. Across this proliferation of names and texts, its function remains constant: it carries out a synthesis of the matter distributed across the first given of Deleuze's system. It "connects" partial objects (AO), "binds" intensities (DR), and "selects" images (C1). The *agent* of this synthesis is the second given Deleuze asks for: the spontaneous imagination (DR), the body without organs (LS, AO), the liquid (LS) or plastic principle (NP).

ONTOLOGY

In *Difference and Repetition*, this synthesis is constitutive of time. This is because the matter which the first synthesis gathers together is characterized by a "rule of discontinuity" or what Deleuze calls, in *What is Philosophy?* and *Expressionism in Philosophy*, "evanescence" (WP 42, 118; EP 201–7). When the first synthesis contracts these passing moments, it carves out an interval in the flow of time and pulls the discontinuous moments into a "living present." It hollows out a "calm and stable center in the heart of chaos" (ATP 311). As Deleuze and Guattari say in *A Thousand Plateaus*, this new-found stability is "in danger of breaking apart at any moment" (ATP 311). This is because the larval subject which performs this synthesis is subject to what Deleuze calls a "contractile finitude" (DR 79): it is capable of retaining only a small number of discontinuous instants and is quickly exhausted and overrun by the relentless passing of instants.[40] The immediate consequence of this is that the larval subject itself passes in time. A second synthesis is, therefore, necessary.

Deleuze calls this second synthesis, the "conjunctive synthesis" (LS), the "disjunctive synthesis" (AO), the "clinch or embrace" (WP 168) "coupling" and "resonance" (DR, FB 73), or affection (C1 62). The name he gives it in *Difference and Repetition* best captures its function: memory. It is a synthesis of reproduction or, as he says in *Anti-Oedipus*, of recording. The body without organs or the passive self takes the elements of the first synthesis and records them on its surface. "The data, the bits of information recorded, and their transmission form a grid of disjunctions of a type that differs from the previous connections" (AO 38). This grid marks out a space of retention which makes the perceptions available for future use.

The third synthesis is simultaneously the most important and the least understood. At a general level though, we can say three things about it. First of all, it proceeds by way of "crisis" (C2), "withdrawal, distension division" (WP 168), castration (LS 206), or an "opening or splitting, hollowing out of sensation" (WP 168). In the third synthesis, the entire system of the passive self "cracks open" (WP 181). Second, this dissolution of the passive self is in part the consequence of a "forced movement" (DR 118; PS 160; LS 239) in which "the limits of sensation are broken, exceeded in all directions" (FB 73). The limits of sensation are broken and exceeded, but this movement does not simply dissolve the self. It "propels us into a new element" (EP 299).

The child of the ritornello "launches forth," Deleuze and Guattari say, in order to join with the "forces of the future" (ATP 311) in a "cosmic becoming" (ATP 311; WP 180). But here we need to draw an important distinction—and this is the third summary thing we can say about this synthesis: this new dimension is not at all identical to the material field from which the passive self emerged. As Deleuze and Guattari say, this cosmic becoming is not the same thing as the chaos from which the child emerged: in the third synthesis, we are indeed ejected from our house, but not "on the side where the old forces of chaos press against it, but in another region, one created by the circle itself."[41] (Likewise, in *Difference and Repetition*, Deleuze will say that any confusion of intensive becoming with virtual or ideal becoming "compromises the whole philosophy of difference" (DR 247).)

The most vivid description of this third synthesis is in *The Logic of Sense* where Deleuze says that this third synthesis represents "the movement by which the ego opens itself to the [metaphysical] surface and liberates the a-cosmic, impersonal, and pre-individual singularities which it had imprisoned. It literally releases them like spores and bursts as it gets unburdened" (LS 213; cf. 222). This is what makes this synthesis so important. It marks the moment at which we leave the confines of the passive self and find ourselves transported to an entirely new level: that of the "metaphysical surface" (LS), the "impersonal transcendental field" (LS 102, PI 25) or "the virtual" (DR 208). It is, therefore, worth describing in considerably more detail that I did for the other syntheses.

Failure

Why is this third synthesis always characterized as a series of cracks, splittings, explosions, shatterings, bursts, or castrations? Or put differently, we know that in this process "sensation" is opened, split, hollowed out, and exceeded in all directions. But it is not immediately clear why sensation would tend, in and of itself, toward its own destruction and failure. In *Coldness and Cruelty* and *Difference and Repetition*, Deleuze sometimes calls this third synthesis the "death instinct" (DR 122, CC 114). But this only names the problem. Why from a genetic point of view does the passive self tend toward its own failure? I want to briefly suggest here (and argue in more detail in Chapters 3 and 4) that this moment constitutes a failure of recognition.

Up until this point, Deleuze's syntheses have closely followed Kant's. The first passive synthesis was a "synthesis of apprehension." It gathered together the matter of the intensive field and bound it into a living present. But because this passive self passed in time, a second synthesis was necessary which took up the bound excitations and recorded them in a space of retention. It thus functioned as a "synthesis of reproduction." At this point in the Kantian model, a third synthesis, the synthesis of recognition, would take over and gather together the apprehended and reproduced representations under the direction of the categories. One could say that the Kantian model requires a guarantee of synthesis, and that this is the function fulfilled by the categories. They are rules for a synthesis of recognition. But because Deleuze is re-writing Kant genetically, he cannot assume that the categories are pre-given. In *Nietzsche and Philosophy*, he is explicit about this: "we require a genesis of reason itself, and also a genesis of the understanding and its categories."[42] What the Deleuzian subject encounters in this third synthesis, then, is a situation in which recognition is called for, but is not guaranteed in advance. It is, therefore, inevitable that synthesis will eventually fail and, as a consequence of this failure, that the subject will find itself awash in optical and sound situations in which it is unable to gather together its representations into a coherent whole and act. But it is precisely at this point, Deleuze says, that we are propelled into a new element. We discover our creative essence—our faculty of "thought" or the virtual—which allows us to create the connection we need to make sense of our situation.

In a fascinating text, Deleuze even suggests that it is possible to manufacture this failure. This is the problem Deleuze's Francis Bacon runs into in his struggle with the cliché:

> But at that very moment once I have begun, how do I proceed so that what I paint does not become a cliché? "Free marks" will have to be made rather quickly on the image being painted so as to destroy the nascent figuration in it . . . .[43]

This is, of course, the opposite situation from the one posed by passive genesis. Whereas the passive self is lacking guidance in the form of categories, Bacon is faced with a surplus of guidance in the form of clichés (or sensory-motor schemata) which he has acquired over the course of his life. But even here, it is only by virtue of a failure of recognition that we discover our creative faculty. It is by virtue of these chance marks that the "diagram" becomes possible. (As I argued in the previous chapter, Deleuze's prose is designed in the same way: it disrupts our habits for making meaning. From this point of view, we could venture a more profound reason for this stylistic device. Rather than simply upsetting convention, he is trying to open up a space in which thought can unroll and think itself beyond the doxa.) Manufactured or not, however, the basic claim here is that this moment of failure marks, as Deleuze and Guattari say in *What is Philosophy?* an *essential* "I do not know" which becomes "positive and creative, the condition of creation itself."[44]

A second problem arises here, though: it is not entirely clear why this failure represents the movement to a new plane and not the simple dissolution of the subject. If we stay within the context of Kant's thought, there are two ways of thinking about this, each specific to Kant's other two Critiques and each characterizing a certain encounter with the abyss. The first draws on the dynamics of the sublime in *The Critique of Judgment*. In the experience of the mathematical sublime, two things happen Kant says. First, the imagination is outstripped by the magnitude of the object or series it is trying to comprehend. It encounters something which is too big for it, and "What is excessive for the imagination . . . is, as it were, an abyss, in which it fears to lose itself."[45] In this failure of apprehension, the imagination recoils on itself. But, at the very moment it finds itself in front of the abyss, "the mind hears in itself the voice of reason."[46] Reason steps into the void and provides the mind with an Idea which easily grasps the magnitude which had eluded the powers of the imagination. At the same time, this gesture reveals a "faculty in the human mind that is itself supersensible."[47]

In this experience, Kant says, "the mind feels itself *moved*."[48] It alternates between the panic of the abyss and the serenity of the supersensible in a kind of "vibration." In the midst of this forced movement, Deleuze points out, reason enters as a kind of "consolation."

[A]t the moment that the imagination finds that it is impotent, no longer able to serve the understanding, it makes us discover in ourselves a still more beautiful faculty which is like the faculty of the infinite. So much so that at the moment we feel for our imagination and suffer with it, since it has become impotent, a new faculty is awakened in us, the faculty of the supersensible.[49]

This logic is clearly at work in the movement from the passive self to that power of thought Deleuze calls "the virtual." But again, the problem with this model is that it presupposes the existence of this other faculty, reason, which lies dormant until awakened. If we are faithful to the question genesis, we have to ask for the genesis of reason in the same way we required the genesis of the understanding and its categories.

In both *Difference and Repetition* and *The Logic of Sense*, Deleuze employs yet another pattern of reasoning to describe this moment, this time from Kant's practical philosophy. Kant held that when I determine an action which meets the requirements of the categorical imperative, that action holds "not merely for men, but for all *rational beings as such*."[50] It does not initially matter, then, that the action I determine might be impossible to perform. We can affirm the practical rule "whether the physical power is sufficient to [it] or not."[51] The categorical imperative puts us in touch with a genuine absolute, or, to use Deleuze's language, it "propels us into a new element." As Kant says, "the moral law ideally *transfers* us into [an intelligible] nature," an "archetypal world" where we take our place in a "system of rational beings."[52]

Deleuze takes up this line of thought in his discussion of the third synthesis in *The Logic of Sense* and *Difference and Repetition*. There he says that in the third synthesis, the subject posits an "action = x," or an "intended action." It is often the case, though, that this action is "too big for me" (DR 89). The Deleuzian subject thus goes through a process similar to the process which the Kantian subject must undergo: after determining an intended act "supposed 'too big for me,'" the subject enters a "present of metamorphosis, a becoming-equal to the act" (DR 89). Up until this point, Deleuze follows Kant closely, but here, he interestingly inverts things. For Deleuze, it is not the intended action (or the act which is too big for me) which propels us into another element as it was for Kant; it is, rather, the "action actually accomplished."

When we pass to the act, a discrepancy arises between the fact of the event, or the outcome of my action, and the projected act (Deleuze's model in *The Logic of Sense* is the Oedipus complex. Intended act: kill your father. Outcome: your castration). This discrepancy seems to give rise to a failure of practical recognition. Both the projected event and the actual act, "turn back against the self which has become their equal and smash it to pieces" (DR 89). Whatever the initial act was, it inevitably leads to this unintended destruction of the self which now constitutes the action "actually accomplished." It is this actually accomplished action—and not the intended action—which propels us into a new element. The "accomplished action is projected onto a surface" Deleuze writes, which is "metaphysical or transcendental" (LS 207). The ego opens itself to the surface and liberates the impersonal and pre-individual singularities which it had imprisoned like spores.

This reversal of Kant, implies a further reversal. For Kant, we momentarily glimpse the intelligible order by vytue of the intended act, even though we remain on the other side of an "infinite unfilled chasm"[53] across which the "holy will"[54] permanently strives. Deleuze's wager in his account of the third synthesis is that we no longer remain on the other side of the abyss. The way in which Deleuze makes the movement from a physical surface to a metaphysical surface, or put differently, the way in which he discovers the passage to the great outdoors, is by affirming the void or abyss rather than trying to traverse it.

In affirming the void between the physical surface and the metaphysical surface, a new power of thought, the aleatory point or the Deleuzian *cogito*, takes shape. "The beginning," Deleuze says, "is truly in the void; it is suspended in the void. It is *with-out*" (LS 218). When recognition fails, we enter a process which Deleuze calls in *The Logic of Sense*, "castration." The phallus, which was the principle of organization in the second synthesis, is lopped off, and in the void which it leaves, we discover a new power: the aleatory point or the "castrated phallus" (LS 218). It is this aleatory point which organizes the singularities released in the dissolution of the passive subject and structures the entire impersonal transcendental field onto which the passive self opens.

The virtual

The metaphysical surface which unfurls in the failure of recognition is called "the virtual" (DR), the "impersonal transcendental field" (LS, PI), the "plane of immanence" (WP), the time-image (C2), the diagram (FB), and so on. It, too, represents a form of becoming, but unlike the becoming of the material field, this is an immaterial and incorporeal becoming. In several texts—most notably, *Difference and Repetition*, *Nietzsche and Philosophy* and *Cinema II*—Deleuze identifies this new surface with the faculty of thought.[55] Unburdened by the constraints of the passive self, the thinker, the "aleatory point," thinks Ideas or "multiplicities"—Ideas which it produces in an ideal, rather than in a passive, synthesis.

The aleatory point is Deleuze's *cogito*, or his I think, eternally returning to its self in an unending process of errant reflection. Unlike the Kantian *cogito*, which Deleuze and Guattari describe as an "ox head wired for sound, which constantly repeats Self = Self,"[56] Deleuze's *cogito* is not concerned with the empty and tautological relation of I with I. It is concerned, rather, with the now dissolved passive self. If the Kantian *cogito* is an I which returns eternally to itself, in an act of reflection, as I[57]; the Deleuzian *cogito* is an I which returns eternally to the dissolved and passive self which is now splayed across the transcendental field.[58] What is more, the Deleuzian *cogito* does not only constantly survey what it *was*; it creates what it *will be*.[59] Deleuze's *cogito* is fundamentally creative: its function is to "survey (WP)," in an ideal synthesis (DR), the "elements" released like spores in the dissolution of the passive self. It establishes connections or "differential relations" between these elements, and it solidifies this structure by creating "singularities (DR)" (now in the mathematical sense of the word). This assemblage of elements, differential relations, and singularities is called an "Idea" (DR, LS), a problem (DR, LS), a "structure" (DI, LS) a "concept" (WP) or a "category of life" (C2). It is what thought thinks.

This is why Deleuze consistently attributes an important genetic function to the aleatory point. In *Difference and Repetition*, it is what "animates" Ideas: it determines the differential relations of an Idea and thereby the singularities which complete the Idea's determination. In *The Logic of Sense*, and "How Do We Recognize Structuralism?," he says that it "animates" structures. In *Cinema II*, it is the ultimate and radical destination of the time-image, a point which organizes the sheets of past, drives the crystal image, and "allocates" the distribution of "differential relations."[60] In *What is Philosophy?* it is the point "in a state of survey" which is at the ground of "concepts," functioning as their principle of organization. In other words, if the essence of thought is creation, the aleatory point names the very locus of creation.

This raises several difficulties for how we understand Deleuze's ontology. The first is related to a question I raised at the beginning of this chapter. This *cogito* marks a paradoxical point in the genesis of the subject: it arises out of the series of passive syntheses and is thus linked directly to a passive subject; at the same time, however, it describes an *impersonal* power of thinking in which this subject now lives. This troubling proximity of the personal and impersonal is not specific to the *Logic of Sense*. In *Difference and Repetition*, we see the same relationship. This power of thought designated by the aleatory point arises out of the failure of the third passive synthesis. It is through this failure that we become the child player of the ideal game and discover our capacity to operate ideal synthesis (DR 198). But to say "our" power here implies that this impersonal transcendental field is somehow personal and capable of being occupied by a child player. Indeed, as I mentioned above, Deleuze clearly considers this capacity to operate an ideal synthesis a *faculty*: the first passive synthesis is the operation of the imagination, the second belongs to memory and the ideal synthesis is operated by "thought."[61] (What is more, the rigor of this connection between the personal and the impersonal is further intensified by the second part of the genesis which I will describe below: the Ideas which thought thinks in its communion with the impersonal are actualized in *my* body.)

Although the passive self dissolves, and although the passive subject, through this dissolution, finds itself thinking in or on an impersonal transcendental field, there is still something uncomfortably personal about it. Deleuze is well aware of this, and the paradox toward which I am pointing is most clearly articulated in one of his last pieces. In "Immanence: A Life. . .," after describing the now oft-quoted scene in Dickens's *Our Mutual Friend*, in which onlookers stare at Rogue Riderhood as he slowly dies, Deleuze explains that what these onlookers saw was not *the* man, but life as such or man as such:

> Between his life and his death, there is a moment that is only that of *a* life playing with death. The life of the individual gives way to an impersonal yet singular life that releases a pure event freed from the accidents of internal and external life, that is from the subjectivity and objectivity of what happens: a 'Homo tantum' with whom everyone empathizes and who attains a sort of beatitude. . . . The life of such individuality fades away in favor of the singular life immanent to a man who no longer has a name, though he can be mistaken for no other. A singular essence, a life. . . .

When we open on to the plane of immanence our individuality fades. Objectivity and subjectivity vanish. We confront impersonality. We no longer have a name. But at the same time we can be mistaken for no other person: our life is "impersonal yet singular." As Dickens remarks, the "spark of life is curiously separable" from Riderhood. Even so, the spark in question is indubitably Riderhood's, and not, for example, the doctor's. The aleatory point is simultaneously our *cogito*, but it does not answer to our name.

There are at least two immediately relevant ways of thinking about the presence of the singular at the level of the absolute. The word "beatitude" here suggests one way in that it directly links this moment to Spinoza. Spinoza's God is composed of singular essences, and each mode expresses one of these essences. Beatitude names that moment at which we, as modes, become fully aware of this fact. Modal essences are impersonal, yet singular. Deleuze's careful discussion of these relationships in *Expressionism in Philosophy* goes a long way toward making this situation clearer, but there is also a larger issue at stake here which potentially complicates this turn to Spinozism, and it turns around the complex question of the unity of substance.

We can (temporarily and purely for the sake of this narrative) avoid the difficulties of this question in Spinoza by turning here to Bergson. Throughout *Creative Evolution*, Bergson develops a distinction between two visions of the Whole—a distinction which Deleuze takes up in *Cinema 1* and *2*. In the first, the absolute is imagined as an "integrally given" Whole characterized by some form of pre-established harmony (Bergson attributes this version to Leibniz and Spinoza); the second is a Whole which is permanently incomplete, fragmented and which "creates itself gradually."[62] Bergson himself tries to merge these two views of the absolute. He wants to think of the absolute as a "harmonious whole," and thus as being in some way unified, but he develops a vision of an imperfect harmony or of a harmony paradoxically characterized by discord:

> the harmony is far from being as perfect as it has claimed to be [in Leibniz's doctrine of pre-established harmony]. It admits of much discord, because each species, each individual even, retains only a certain impetus from the universal vital impulsion and tends to use its energy in its own interest.[63]

The unity of this vital impulsion is merely retrospective.[64] It is "rather behind us than before."[65] "Life does not proceed," Bergson argues, "by the association and addition of elements, but by dissociation and division,"[66] and as a consequence, "Roads may fork or by-ways be opened along which dissociated elements may evolve in an independent manner. . . ."[67] This second, fragmented and divided whole is nonetheless a kind of whole. Each species and each individual carries with it a bit of the original spark of life—and "it is in virtue of the primitive impetus of the whole that the movement of the parts continues."[68] But even so, life as it currently stands is no longer in possession of a thorough-going unity, and it is thus dependent on the individuals and species across which it travels. As Bergson constantly emphasizes, his vision of the Whole is that of a finite, divided, and incomplete God—a God which "creates itself gradually."[69] Bergson's God, Deleuze writes in *Bergsonism*, is an "open and finite God."[70]

Deleuze develops this line of thought in *Cinema 1* and *2*, and it receives its most substantial development across his discussion of the aleatory point in *Cinema 2*. Here, he takes on Bergson's distinction between two Wholes. The first is a "continuous" whole, characterized by a rational coherence and the commensurability of all points within it (C2 181). This is the whole which much of *Cinema 1* was concerned with. But when the aleatory point comes on the scene in *Cinema 2*, Deleuze says this earlier vision of the absolute is no longer functional. And not only is it not functional, it is no longer even enough to say that the whole is "open" as Deleuze himself had said in *Bergsonism*. The statement "the whole was the open" needs to be replaced with "the whole is the outside" (C2 179). This second vision of the whole is a vision of a cracked whole, characterized by what Deleuze called in *The Logic of Sense* "alogical incompatibilities" and "noncausal correspondences."[71] It is a "chaosmos." In *Cinema 2*, it is characterized as a "sequence of irrational points" and "non-chronological time relationships" (181).

When we rethink the absolute in these terms—as emerging from the void or the outside, we completely change its nature. It is no longer a unified substance which communicates across its parts to infinity. Deleuze writes that

> The whole undergoes a mutation, because it has ceased to be One-Being, in order to become the constitutive 'and' of things, the constitutive between-two of images. Thus the whole merges with that [sic.] Blanchot calls the force of 'dispersal of the Outside', or 'the vertigo of spacing': that void which is no longer a motor-part of the image, and which the image would cross in order to continue, but is the radical calling into question of the image. (C2 180)

This passage recapitulates in a condensed form most of the themes relating to the aleatory point I have separated out. We can notice first of all that this whole emerges from a void, an infinite unfilled chasm. Second, that this void is characterized by a break with passivity (or the sensory-motor system) and that this break is initiated by a radical calling into question of the images this sensory-motor system gathered together. As Deleuze says in the pages following this one, this new whole "determines," "creates," "allocates," or "a*nimates*" the "differential relations" contained within the "categories of life."

The main point I want this passage to make, however, is that this new whole is radically different than the infinite of the classical philosophers with which this chapter began. *Cinema 2* was published in 1985. If we return to the 1980 Leibniz lecture I quoted at the beginning of this chapter, we can see the kind of reversal that Deleuze is pointing toward here. When he contrasted the classical philosophers—which began innocently with the infinite—to philosophy after Kant, he very quietly changed the sense of the infinite. When we begin from finitude, infinity takes on a new meaning:

> The finite will no longer be a limitation of the infinite; rather, the infinite will be an overcoming [dépassement] of the finite. . . . The infinite is no longer separable from an act of overcoming finitude.[72]

The infinite is now a process of self-transcendence and nothing more.[73] It becomes the *constitutive* "and" of things. "Substance," Deleuze says in a 1956 essay on Bergson is, "alteration."[74] But alteration here does not mean becoming in general. Nor does it meant that our identity is determined by our difference from all other things. Deleuze is clear that it means our capacity to differ from *ourselves*. It is this capacity that constitutes our reality and accomplishes "the unity of substance and subject."[75] He makes this claim in a different way at the end of *Difference and Repetition*. In this new vision of the whole, modes no longer turn around substance, substance turns around the modes. The absolute is our capacity to differ from ourselves and to transcend ourselves. What we discover in the aleatory point is our creative potential, or our power of self-transcendence as such.

This reading is further confirmed, if we consider the mode of approach to the absolute. We do not form a rational Idea which God also thinks; there is no logical regression through conditions to an anhypothetical principle; we do not enter into a mystical experience (though Deleuze does say there is a sober approach); we do not glimpse it in the lightning flash of wit; we do not reconstruct a fictional but necessary representation; nor do we approach it through the unfolding of a (symmetrical) dialectic. We approach the absolute through failure. We experience it when we attempt to think an encounter without the guidance of already-made concepts, pregiven categories, or the guidance of past experience. We approach it when we affirm an encounter by creating an Idea which is adequate to it and it alone.

The static genesis

The static genesis is a process which is best known as "actualization" or "individuation." It is the second broad movement of Deleuze's thought. If the dynamic genesis moved from the material flux up to the faculty of thought through a series of passive and progressive syntheses, here we move in the opposite direction—from the virtual back to the actual. If the first movement was Deleuze's replaying of the Kantian syntheses, this one is his replaying of the schematism. There has been a strong tendency in Deleuze studies to imagine this process as a more or less univocal determination of the actual by the virtual, as though the actual arose mysteriously from the virtual. In fact, it is a complex redeployment of the passive self and its passive syntheses in accordance with the requirements of the Idea.

Dramatization/schematism

The static genesis begins with what Deleuze calls in *Difference and Repetition*, "dramatization." He explicitly links this concept to Kant's schematism, and it works in essentially the same way. The general problem of the schematism was how to carry conceptual relations—and in particular those of the categories—into the realm of sensibility. How do you get from conceptual determinations to spatiotemporal determinations? For Kant, and especially for Deleuze's Kant, it is through an act of the imagination—an "inventive act of the imagination"—which is "capable of indicating the condition under which individual cases are subsumed under the concept."[76] Schemata are not images despite being products of the imagination, Deleuze says. A schema consists, rather, in "*spatio-temporal relations which embody or realize relations which are in fact conceptual.*"[77] In *What is Philosophy?*, in their "machinic portrait of Kant," Deleuze and Guattari imagine schemata turning on a wheel which plunges in an out of "the shallow stream of time."[78] What happens when these schemata are plunged back into time is made admirably clear by Béatrice Longuenesse. Schemata, she shows, are rules for synthesis.[79] They function by directing each of the syntheses.

In Deleuze, at this point, we are in an analogous situation. If Kant had to move from concepts to the forms of sensibility, Deleuze has to move from Ideas back to the field of intensity from which they emerged. Deleuze's Ideas, though, are not ideas of *possible* objects or of classes of objects. They are Ideas of *singular* objects. They account for the problem Deleuze claimed Kant avoided in passage of *Kant's Critical Philosophy* quoted above: Deleuze's Ideas constitute "the *particular* laws of this or that object."[80] Similarly, intensity, Deleuze's form of sensibility, is not characterized by the empty forms of space and time, but by material flows which affect the passive subject in a great number of ways. There is, then, a concreteness and an immediacy to Deleuze's vision of this process which is not there in Kant (and which Kant rigorously tried to remove). Even so, the process by which Deleuze traverses the space between Ideas and intensity, dramatization, works in analogous way. It "immediately incarnates the differential relations, the singularities and the progressivities immanent in the Idea."[81]

In *what* are these Ideas incarnated? Immediately following this passage, Deleuze writes that "every Idea turns us into larvae." "Shining points pierce us." Larvae, "bear Ideas in their flesh." Ideas "mobilize and compromise *the whole body*."[82] Dramatization returns to the body and to the order of the passive self. It inscribes Ideas in our flesh. In doing so, however, it radically reshapes the body. If Deleuze's images here all evoke some kind of shimmering violence, it is because dramatization brings the rules of the Idea to bear on the passive processes of larval subjects. In other words, in the same way that the Kantian schematism worked by co-opting the imagination's synthesis, the Deleuzian drama returns to the body and redirects its syntheses.

A passive synthesis, I said above, is one which is not rule-governed. These same syntheses under the influence of ideal relations, then, are no longer passive, but active.

Active synthesis

Deleuze's doctrine of active synthesis is one of the least studied aspects of his thought. I merely want to trace the contours of this process here. It has two distinct stages: "good sense" and "common sense."

Good sense fixes limits. As he says in *The Logic of Sense*, good sense is essentially "agricultural, inseparable from the agrarian problem, the establishment of enclosures."[83] It "territorializes" (AO). This territorialization bears on both subjects and objects. It transforms the "indeterminate object" into a "this or that," and it "individualizes" a determinate "self."[84] Good sense is a "quantitative synthesis of difference" (DR 226), Deleuze writes. It cancels intensity, binds it, and transforms it into "extensity," thus giving it spatial coordinates it never had in the intensive flux. What I want to emphasize here, however, is that it does this by taking over the first passive synthesis and submitting its operations to the rules contained in the Idea: "Good sense is based upon a synthesis of time, in particular the one we have determined as the first synthesis, that of habit."[85] This is even more developed in *Anti-Oedipus* where Deleuze and Guattari show that the territorial stage of social production functions by co-opting all three of the passive syntheses.

This initial cancellation of difference is not sufficient to constitute an object, and at this point, a second synthesis takes over. A second "active synthesis is established on the foundation of the passive syntheses: this consists in relating the bound excitation to an object supposed to be both real and the end of our actions."[86] This is the synthesis of "common sense" which relates the excitations to an object and to a subject. (In *Anti-Oedipus*, it works by submitting desiring-production to the "body of the despot" (AO) and the "Urstaat" (AO), the object-form and the subject-form, respectively.[87]) Common sense is a "qualitative synthesis of diversity, the static synthesis of qualitative diversity related to an object supposed the same for all the faculties of a single subject."[88] In other words, common sense relates diversity—the manifold—to an individuated object and to an individuated subject. And like good sense, it operates by subjecting the passive self to the guidance of an Idea.[89]

Unlike the passive syntheses which were successive and incapable of functioning together, by virtue of the Idea they incarnate the active syntheses work together and depend on one another. Whereas common sense relates bound excitations to an object, it points back to good sense, a "dynamic instance, capable of determining the indeterminate object as this or that, and of individualizing the self situated in this ensemble of objects."[90] But good sense can only perform this function insofar as the second active synthesis, common sense, is already operative.

However, precisely because it ensures the distribution of that difference in such a manner that it tends to be cancelled in the object, and because it provides a rule according to which the different objects tend to equalize themselves and the different Selves tend to become uniform, good sense in turn points toward the instance of common sense which provides it with both the form of a universal Self and that of an indeterminate object.

If this harmonious relation between the two active syntheses is possible, it is because the Idea establishes what Klossowski calls "a precarious armistice" among the faculties of the passive self.[91] In the process of dramatization, the Idea allocates "roles" to the various faculties allowing them to carry out the processes of actualization and individuation though which they relate bound excitations to object forms.

Representation

This genetic line ends in representation— in the "object supposed to be both real and the end of our actions."[92] Every object, Deleuze says, is defined by two things: "the quality or qualities which it possesses, the extension which it occupies."[93] These two characteristics—quality and extensity—are the basic "elements of representation."[94] They are the central coordinates of the "perceptual world."[95] The basic units of "propositions of consciousness."

Unlike the unindividuated matter at the foundation of this genesis—which is in a state of permanent becoming (characterized by intensive relationships)—and unlike the flow of the virtual— whose elements are also submerged in a flow of becoming (now characterized by differential relationships)—representations have well-defined borders. They are capable of being put alongside one another. They occupy a spatial extensity. In addition to this, they also possess a quality or qualities. Both of these characteristics draw their power from the virtual Idea. In the process of actualization, the singularities shape the matter of perception (intensity) into extensive parts; the rhythm of the differential relations determines the object's quality. In the same way that the plastic principle at the foundation of this genesis molded itself to the conditions of its emergence, and in the same way that the Idea created in thought remained adequate to immediate state of affairs out of which it arose, the object individuated here is a singular object. This object might indeed ground what we normally think of as repetition, Deleuze argues. Its extensity allows us to think equivalence and its quality allows us to think of resemblance. And what's more, this interplay of equivalence and resemblance makes the formation of concepts possible. But Deleuze is not concerned with any of this. What he is interested in is the way in which a singular representation can emerge from a given state of affairs.

It is in this context that Deleuze draws an important distinction between two kinds of representations: living and dead. In *The Logic of Sense*, he puts it this way: "two types of knowledge have often been distinguished, one indifferent remaining external to its object, and the other concrete, seeking its object wherever it is" (LS 146).

> Representation attains this topical ideal only by means of the hidden expression which it encompasses, that is, by means of the event it envelops. There is thus a 'use' of representation without which representation would remain lifeless and senseless.[96]

This distinction appears across Deleuze's *oeuvre* in various disguises. In *Difference and Repetition*, it is a question of representations caught up in the other-structure (and thus expressive, by virtue of a halo, of their virtual origins) and of representations which have been cut off from this structure (DR 260–61). In *Francis Bacon*, it is the difference between the "figure" and the "cliché": the figure, capable of providing an intuitive interpretation of the thing itself and the cliché, a dead, lifeless representation which always intervenes between the thing and its reality.[97] In either case what is at stake is the difference between what we might call "a legitimate and illegitimate use of representation." Representations are capable of legitimate use when they remain tied to the conditions of their emergence; they are capable of illegitimate use when they are cut off from this source. "Representation, when it does not reach this point remains only a dead letter confronting that which it represents, and stupid in its representiveness" (LS 146).

3

Ethics

Reason, strength and freedom are in Spinoza inseparable from a development, a formative process, a culture. Nobody is born free, nobody is born reasonable. And nobody can undergo for us the slow learning of what agrees with our nature, the slow effort of discovering our joys.[1]

Joy is man's passage from a lesser to a greater perfection.[2]

Deleuze's ethics build on the subject at the foundation of his ontology which I outlined in the previous chapter. They are concerned not with our responsibility, infinite or otherwise, to the Other, but with the organization of a life and with the course of a life's development. For this reason, I will argue that his ethics are best thought of as a kind of perfectionism. They are perfectionist in the sense that the good is what brings us toward greater perfection. But this perfectionism comes with a major qualification: there is no one end, or even a collection of ends, which functions as a focal point or terminus and which might, therefore, determine what counts as perfect. This is because our "essence" is fundamentally creative of new possibilities for life. Deleuze's ethics, you could say, constitute a perfectionism without a concept of the perfect.[3]

The main effort of this chapter, however, is to show that Deleuze's discussion of ethics in Spinoza and Nietzsche can be legitimately carried over to Deleuze's own thought, and my argument here turns on the way in which, through a structural monotony, *Expressionism in Philosophy* and *Nietzsche and Philosophy* replay the central concepts of Deleuze's other works. Both texts take up and rethink the basic moments of subjectivity outlined in the previous chapter. The most important of these texts is *Expressionism in Philosophy*, and it is with that text that I begin.

Deleuze's Spinoza

In a letter to Martin Joughin, the translator of *Expressionism in Philosophy*, Deleuze remarked that what interested him most in Spinoza was not Spinoza's conception of substance, "but the composition of finite modes." "I consider this," Deleuze wrote, "one of the most original aspects of my book."[4] My contention in the first part of this chapter is that if we closely follow the evolution of the third part of *Expressionism in Philosophy* in which Deleuze develops this theory of finite modes, we can witness Deleuze gently pushing Spinoza in the direction of Deleuze's own account of subjectivity.[5] If this is interesting, it is because at the same time Deleuze undertakes this buggery, he develops important ethical positions which we might be able to carry over to, and treat as representative of, Deleuze's own thought. It should be obvious then, but it is still worth saying, that what I am concerned with here is not Deleuze's reading of Spinoza *as* a reading of Spinoza. I am well aware that the moments of the text I highlight are occasionally marginal and that sometimes I emphasize those aspects which make them even less typical. What I am concerned with is locating that place of structural monotony in which we can see Deleuze thinking with or through Spinoza.

The "properly ethical question" of *Expressionism in Philosophy* asks how the body can "become active."[6] While it may be obvious, it is worth saying that if the ethical question asks how we might become active, the implication of this question and the starting point for Deleuze's inquiry, is that the body is not yet active. The ethical question is posed specifically in terms of the body and its passivity, and thus the answer to this question—how does one become active?—is going to involve a genesis, "a development, a formative process, a culture."[7] We have to clarify at the outset, then, the initial situation of this genesis and in particular the specific meaning Deleuze gives to the two constraints at the heart of it: body and passivity.

The body is a certain *arrangement* of "extensive parts," Deleuze says. This arrangement—the body's "characteristic relation"—is not defined by the parts or even by functional groupings of parts (e.g. the organs). It is characterized by the body's "individual form,"[8] or its "structure"[9]: the body is "a system of relations between the parts of the body (these parts not being organs, but the anatomical parts of those organs)."[10] The words "form" and "structure" connote rigidity, but this form is neither static nor rigid. "The relation that characterizes an existing mode as a whole is endowed with a kind of elasticity,"[11] Deleuze writes. And at the beginning of Chapter 14, Deleuze identifies the body's structure with "power." A body's characteristic relation, its structure, or its form is identical to that body's capacity to be affected. The two are interchangeable according to a "strict order of equivalences." This identification lets us rephrase the "properly ethical question" in two ways:

> [Characteristic] relations are inseparable from the capacity to be affected. So that Spinoza can consider two fundamental questions as equivalent: *What is the structure (fabrica) of a body?* And: *What can a body do?* A body's structure is the composition of its relation. What a body can do corresponds to the nature and limits of its capacity to be affected.[12]

The implication of this double question is that the body is not a static form, but a dynamic or plastic form. It is a form that is subject to affections, some of which agree with it and some of which disagree, and it internalizes these affections and is modified by them.

"Passivity" in this context refers to the body's total immersion in the set of extensive parts. Taken as a whole, the nature of extensive parts "is such that they 'affect one another' *ad infinitum*," and because a mode is itself an assemblage of extensive parts, "one may infer that an existing mode is affected in a very great number of ways."[13] The body is itself an assemblage of extensive parts, and these parts, too, communicate with other parts to infinity according to the laws governing movement and rest. From the point of view of the body involved, however, these encounters can only appear as "chance encounters." Affections, from this perspective, are "brutal, violent and fortuitous."[14] Existing modes are "determined and affected from the outside, *ad infinitum*. Every existing mode is thus inevitably affected by modes external to it, and undergoes changes that are not explained by its own nature alone. Its affections are, at the outset, and tend to remain passions."[15]

The first point of comparison we can make with Deleuze's other texts then, is to notice that this starting point—the body in its passivity—does not significantly depart from the original position I outlined in the previous chapter. If we momentarily adopt, for the sake of comparison, the language of the *Logic of Sense*, we can observe that what he called the "primary order" in that text, the place at which the entire dynamic genesis of sense (and, from there, the static genesis of representation) began, is defined in exactly this way: the body without organs, a passive ego, finds itself dissolved in a sea of partial objects like a drop of wine in the ocean.[16] If this ego is passive, it is because it has no control over its affections, and Deleuze, in this latter text, is explicit about the violence this entails. There are aggressive interjections, projections, and splittings that the body without organs is subject to.[17]

In addition, this notion of the plasticity of form here seems to meet the basic requirements Deleuze identified in his characterization of the kind of principle which could adequately account for Kantian synthesis—namely, that it be "an essentially *plastic* principle that is no wider than what it conditions, that changes itself with the conditioned and determines itself in each case along with what it determines."[18] In *Nietzsche and Philosophy*, this principle was called the "will to power." In *Expressionism in Philosophy*, is the body's power, its capacity to be affected.

This is the operative concept in the genetic program sketched below. Of the numerous consequences of such a concept, one which is worth emphasizing at the start is that modifications of the body's structure do not result in merely mechanical or quantitative changes to the form. The affections or modifications of modes consist "not only of mechanical changes in the affections it experiences, but also dynamic changes in the capacity to be affected and in 'metaphysical' changes of their essence itself."[19] There are thus qualitative or "metaphysical" shifts at certain points which have the potential to bring an assemblage under an entirely new essence. This is the reason we does not know what a body can do. It is not because we have not come to terms with the details of its reality through exhaustive empirical study. It is because it can enter into new relations with new prostheses which completely change its nature.[20]

Genesis

The properly ethical question is asked from the point of view of this conceptual constellation then: the body, understood as a dynamic form subject to affections beyond its control. It is in these conditions that we ask "Can a mode attain to active affections, and, if so, how?"[21] There are two different ways in which Deleuze describes this process of becoming-active.

One is through an economy of joyful and sad passions. When we feel pleasure, our power of life is augmented, and when we feel pain, it is diminished. The task of becoming active on this account is to maximize joyful passions and minimize sad ones, *so that* we might eventually be able to liberate ourselves from the passions altogether. This end—liberation from the passions, whether joyful or sad—is essential. It is what prevents Spinoza's ethics from becoming either a purely hedonistic ethics or a quantitative calculus of the greatest happiness. Joy is pursued not for itself, but for the perfection, freedom, and beatitude which might result from it.[22]

The second way Deleuze describes this process is through a consistent emphasis on faculty psychology. The formative process by which we become active takes place across the successive development or cultivation of the faculties. We move from an order of encounters, which we might call (though Deleuze does not) "an original sensibility," to imagination, memory, understanding, and finally to reason. In my brief sketch of the genesis of activity below, I am going to focus on this faculty psychology for two reasons. The first is that this attention to faculty psychology is characteristic of many of Deleuze's texts, from *Proust and Signs* to *Difference and Repetition*. Paying attention to its structure and function here, thus, makes it much easier to draw connections with those other texts (though I will not explicitly make these connections here).

The second reason is that the process of development has important consequences for how we understand the economy of joyful and sad passions. Not only does this economy have a determinate end as mentioned above (the freedom from the passions altogether), but the fact that we move from one faculty to the next means that pleasure does not accumulate in an additive way.[23] One does not just add pleasure to pleasure to pleasure. Rather, at certain points in the process, there is a qualitative shift, a "genuine leap,"[24] whereby one moves from imagination to understanding to reason. By focusing on the doctrine of faculties, then, we automatically avoid any easy quantitative reading of joy. Each faculty brings with it a different way of knowing, and thus "different ways of living, different modes of existing."[25] Joy is not an end in itself, rather it is merely the means by which we move toward greater perfection.

Imagination and memory

The "formative process," or the genetic line at the end of which reason is born, begins at the level of the body, a plastic form, dissolved in the "common order of nature" and subject to fortuitous encounters with other bodies. The first faculty to be born in this situation is the imagination. Although this is the lowest faculty of the soul, it receives the most complex and difficult discussion in Deleuze's text. There are several characteristics of this faculty that I want to separate out here, in large part because they create important links with Deleuze's other texts (and primarily with *Difference and Repetition* and *The Logic of Sense*).

The first is its moment of production. The imagination is produced in the encounter between two bodies, our body and another body. This encounter, however, has to be of a certain type. The body that we encounter must "agree" with ours. It is only in this situation that the effect of the encounter is joy, and it is only through the pleasure we experience in a joyful encounter that the imagination is bodied forth. Here is the central passage: "Insofar as the feeling of joy increases our power of action, it determines us to desire, imagine, do, all we can in order to preserve this joy itself and the object that procures it for us."[26] When we undergo a joyful encounter, we desire to prolong the affection, and this transforms our desire into an imagining. Joy is characterized here by its effect: a joyful encounter creates the desire to *preserve* the cause of that joy (the object that we have encountered). This is, in part, why the faculty to be born at this stage is the imagination: it is the faculty which presents its object whether or not that object is present.[27]

Deleuze immediately considers the contrary case—when we are affected by a body which does not agree with ours—and it reveals the same conclusion from the opposite point of view: only joyful affections lead to the production of the imagination. When we are affected by bodies which do not agree with ours, nothing positive happens: the "sadness is not added to the desire that follows from it: rather, the desire is inhibited by this feeling . . . ."[28] If the imagination is born of our desire to prolong the pleasurable affection—we imagine a joyful object to be present even when it is not—sadness leads to precisely the opposite situation. Rather than desiring to prolong the affection, we try to cut it short.

The second characteristic of the imagination I want to highlight here follows more or less obviously from the first. If the imagination emerges in the joyful encounter of two bodies, it has something like a perceptive capacity. Within the context of a discussion of the three types of knowledge, Deleuze writes that the "first kind (imagination)" corresponds to "the state of nature: I *perceive* objects through chance encounters, and by the effect they have on me."[29] Forty pages earlier, when explaining just what made this lowest kind of knowledge so low, Deleuze explained that passive affections, whether joyful or sad, "cut us off from that which we are capable, *this is because our power of action is reduced to attaching itself to their traces*, either in the attempt to preserve them if they are joyful, or to ward them off if they are sad."[30] This is the second function of the imagination, then. It attaches itself to the "traces" which encounters leave behind. It gathers those traces together and desires to prolong the joyful ones.

These first two characteristics taken together imply the third and final characteristic which Deleuze attributes to the imagination (which I will address here): the imagination has a specific temporality. An affection indicates "the *present* constitution of our own body, and so the way in which our capacity to be affected is being at that moment exercised. An affection of our body is only a corporeal image, and the idea of the affection as it is in our mind an inadequate idea, an imagining."³¹ The imagination is a synthesis of apprehension which limits itself to the present in time. It "indicates the present state of our body's constitution." It is precisely the temporality of the imagination—its grounding in the present—which is its weakness and which causes us to move on to the next faculty, memory. Deleuze's argument is as follows: "[W]hile our body exists, it endures, and is defined by duration; its present state is thus inseparable from a previous state with which it is linked in a continuous duration."³² Imagination does not record these alterations. Memory does: "*to every idea that indicates an actual state of our body* [i.e. imaginings], *there is necessarily linked another sort of idea that involves the relation of this state to the earlier state.*"³³ While Deleuze does not actually name the faculty of this reproductive synthesis here, it is obvious that it is memory for two reasons. The first is simply its function: it relates the present to an earlier state. The second reason is that when he finally names it ninety pages later, it is exactly in the same context. The "imagination corresponds to the actual imprint of some body in our own, and memory to the succession of imprints in time. Memory and imagination are true parts of the soul."³⁴

Deleuze talks about the faculty of memory only twice, and on the first occasion, he does not even name it. Despite its marginality, however, it plays a crucial role in the text. Each time it appears, it appears as a temporal synthesis. The imagination is knowledge of the present, but because we endure in time, those presents pass. The importance of this for my argument, however, is again the connections it allows us to make with Deleuze's other texts. We might notice, for example, that the role Deleuze very briefly attributes to memory here accords with the role of memory in *Difference and Repetition*. In the second chapter of *Difference and Repetition* (in which Deleuze develops his theory of the passive syntheses), the first synthesis—of the imagination—carves out a living present by binding the intensities scattered across the sensible field, but this passive synthesis passes in time. We, thus, need a second passive synthesis, that of memory, to ground the first. Deleuze's account of imagination and memory in *Expressionism in Philosophy*, then, clearly resonates with the problems of passive synthesis in *Difference and Repetition*.

The next moment of the genesis only reinforces this set of parallel connections I am drawing. Understanding appears as a kind of synthesis of recognition which stands on the work of imagination and memory and tries to unite the two.

Understanding and reason

The understanding is born with the first "common notion." "When we form a common notion, our soul is said 'to use reason:' we come into possession of our power of action or of understanding."[35] The question is how this is possible if we are given over to chance from the moment we are born. Deleuze explains the genesis of the understanding this way:

> Everything about existence condemned us to having only inadequate ideas: we had ideas neither of ourselves, nor of external bodies, but only ideas of affections, indicating the effect of some external body on us. But precisely from such an effect we can form the idea of what is common to some external body and our own.[36]

There are two things we might notice here. The first is that the first common notions we form are of those things which we directly encounter in our daily experience. These local encounters, Deleuze will continue to insist, must be joyful. Common notions—and thus the faculty which thinks them—do not arise from painful encounters, but like the imagination, only from joyful encounters. "Sadness, which arises from our encounter with a body that does not agree with ours, never incites us to form a common notion; but joy-passion, as an increase of the power of acting and of comprehending, does bring this about: it is an occasional cause of the common notion."[37]

Second, we might also notice that Deleuze is arguing that common notions are built on the foundation of the first kind of knowledge. The imagination gave us the "idea of affections." It attached itself to traces, and indicated the "effect of some external body on us." As Deleuze says in the passage above it is "from such an effect we can form the idea of what is common to some external body and our own." In other words, the origin of the understanding is not the order of encounters, but the order of imagination and memory: "common notions find in imagination the very conditions of their formation."[38]

If common notions represent our first foray into an active life, it is because we extract from our affections—or better, we create—something which was never in images or traces—namely the idea of something common between two bodies. The idea of something common thus flows from *us* and not from our encounters. If we wanted to stretch this (and I realize this is a stretch), we might say that common notions, then, are formed on the basis of a comparison between two imaginings, one present and one reproduced. The understanding is built on the synthesis of imagination (or apprehension) with memory (or reproduction).

The next step in this genetic line is the birth of reason as such. This raises the immediate question of the nature of the distinction between reason and understanding. Often the two are used interchangeably in Deleuze's text. To say "reason" and to say "understanding" amounts to more or less the same thing for most of *Expressionism in Philosophy*. But late in the text it becomes clear that Deleuze is working with a functional distinction between the two faculties. Both understanding and reason belong to the same power—our essence or power of activity—but the understanding is applied to objects of experience (imaginings or perceptions), whereas reason forms concepts which do not have a correlate in experience, the idea of God for example: "The idea of God is in a sense opposed to common notions in that they always apply to things that can be imagined, while God cannot be imagined."[39] Put only slightly differently, the understanding forms concepts which can be applied to experience. Reason forms concepts under which all experience belongs but which can never be an object of experience or Ideas.[40]

What is most interesting about this moment of Deleuze's text, however, is that this split causes the process of formation itself to split. This new kind of knowledge, Reason, "propels us into a new element"[41] in which we attain a "direct vision" of the infinite.[42] But once we have ascended from imagination to reason on this genetic line, we does not stay perched at the top in a kind of disinterested contemplation of pure ideas. Rather, the ideas we think and the common notions we create need to be "applied" to the body.

Schematism?

"Reason in its initial development" Deleuze says, is "the effort to organize encounters on the basis of perceived agreements and disagreements."[43] But why would Reason, which propels us into a new element, return to the order of encounters? Deleuze even argues that this effort to return heightens the more rational or active we become. To become active implies a continuous return to the order of fortuitous encounters and passive affections—a return in which we organize those encounters rationally. Through our activity we become capable of ordering the affections of the body according to our essence: we "have the power of ordering and connecting the affections of the body according to the order of the understanding."[44]

Deleuze is insistent on this. Throughout this section of the text (EP 204–96), he consistently uses the verb "to apply" to refer to the action by which common notions return to the body and organize its affections rationally. Twice Deleuze strengthens the verb and says that common notions "impose themselves on the imagination."[45] This gives us a better idea of what he means by "application." By means of this imposition, common notions "*intervene in the movement of imagination, and divert its course to their own ends.*"[46]

This notion that the understanding intervenes in the functioning of the imagination and even co-opts its movement for its own ends is nowhere, to my knowledge, in Spinoza. There is some loose textual evidence for it in *Ethics* V.7p and V.10s, but Deleuze is clearly stretching Spinoza at this point. This is made more apparent by the fact that Deleuze abandons this interpretation in his discussion of common notions in *Spinoza: Practical Philosophy*. In this later text, he mentions the complex relation between common notions and imagination, reaffirming that common notions are born of imaginings and fold back on the imagination, and there is still a secret harmony between the two faculties. But this return to the imagination is no longer an application by which the very movement of the imagination is diverted to the ends of the understanding. Rather, common notions simply explain by an internal principle what the imagination grasped externally.[47]

I would argue that it is through *this* particular torsion that we can see Deleuze thinking through the problems of *Difference and Repetition* in

Expressionism in Philosophy. "To apply" is one of the verbs Kant used in the *Critique of Pure Reason* to characterize the schematism, and it is the one Deleuze consistently used in his commentaries on Kant: a schema is what allows us *to apply* concepts of the understanding to sensibility.[48] One could even go so far as to say that insofar as the schema is the act of the *imagination* which makes this application possible, in the schematism, the understanding works by intervening in the movement of the imagination and directing its course to its own ends.[49]

While this theory of "application" is difficult to find Spinoza, it is a central feature of *Difference and Repetition* (as I argued in the previous chapter) where Deleuze rewrites the Kantian schematism as "dramatization." This process is operated by what he calls there "spatio-temporal dynamisms." These dynamisms, he says, are the "actualizing, differenciating agents."[50] They are what set off the entire process of actualization *by applying virtual Ideas to the intensities sensible field*. They thus cross the gap between two asymmetrical faculties. The only way in which actualization takes place, however, is if these dynamisms can co-opt the passive syntheses. One could say that the passive syntheses are *diverted* from their passive functioning by these dynamisms and begin to synthesize according to the rules laid out by virtual Ideas.[51] In this way, they become active syntheses ("good sense" and "common sense") which move us from the virtual to the level of representation.

We might then, on the basis of all of these comparisons, draw up the following table:

Expressionism in philosophy	Difference and repetition
1 Extensive Parts	1 Intensity (Sensibility)
2 Imagination	2 First Passive Synthesis (of Imagination)
3 Memory	3 Second Passive Synthesis (of Memory)
4 Understanding	4 Third Passive Synthesis (of Thought)
5 Reason	5 Virtual
6 'Application'	6 Dramatization
7 Diversion of Imagination	7 Active Synthesis

Set out schematically like this, the resemblances and the differences between the conceptual structures of each text both become especially sharp. The most important difference, and the one which will prevent us from immediately deriving a Deleuzian ethics from *Expressionism*, is number five: Rationality and Virtuality. While both involve the active production of Ideas, Spinozan rationality and Deleuzian virtuality are not at all equivalent faculties. The movement from the one to the other is, I will argue below, what is at stake in Deleuze's reading of Nietzsche. Before we get to Deleuze's ethics, then, we have to move beyond Spinoza. In the same way that Nietzsche overtakes Spinoza as the thinker of immanence in *Difference and Repetition* (40–1), we need to transcend Spinoza's conception of human essence here.[52]

From reason to thought

At the heart of *Nietzsche and Philosophy* is the same problem Deleuze worked through in the third part of *Expressionism in Philosophy*: how does one become active. And again, this takes place through a complex genesis. I does not want to trace this formative process in anything like the detail I did for *Expressionism in Philosophy* for several reasons, not the least of which is that one consequence of Deleuze's monotony is that I have already covered this process on multiple occasions, so I can contain it here within a few paragraphs.

The original position in *Nietzsche and Philosophy* is much the same as it is in all of his other texts; in fact it is at this level—that of the origin—that Deleuze first asserts the similarity between Spinoza and Nietzsche.[53] Here, too, we find an originary subjectivity which is beset by its affections. These affections are called "forces" and this subjectivity is called alternatively "the body" (as defined by a characteristic relation[54]) or "the will to power," both of which Deleuze characterizes as a "capacity for being affected."[55] Sometimes he calls it a "sensibility,"[56] but ultimately it should be understood as a "principle of synthesis of forces"[57] characterized by its "plasticity."[58] Like the Spinozist body, this principle is determined by what it determines and vice versa.[59]

Deleuze is very clear that this synthesis of forces in the will to power is a rethinking of the Kantian syntheses (it is precisely this, Deleuze says, which guarantees that "Nietzsche belongs to the history of Kantianism"[60]). The will to power performs two basic syntheses. The first is a "synthesis of diversity" (*le divers*). "*Le divers*" is the French word used to translate Kant's *das Mannigfaltige*, or what we read in English as the sensible "manifold." This first synthesis thus roughly corresponds with Kant's synthesis of apprehension. It runs through and gathers together the forces which affect the will, or what Deleuze refers to later in the text (and in a Freudian idiom) as "excitations."[61] The second synthesis is "the reproduction of diversity," and it functions by automatically retaining "mnemonic traces" of excitations.[62] It thus corresponds, roughly, to Kant's synthesis of reproduction. (As Deleuze indirectly points out, each of these syntheses is a temporal synthesis—the first relates to the present in time and the second to the past.[63]) But at this stage, a problem develops, for the will to power very quickly becomes reactive.[64] Rather than attaching itself to excitations, it ties itself to traces which separate the body from what it can do. They distract it and link its reactions not only to prior actions, but also to the incoming traces, thus creating a purely reactive animal. It is the third synthesis which solves this problem and which we are interested in here.

This third synthesis, which Deleuze calls "the eternal return," has two aspects: a theoretical one and a practical one.[65] Theoretically, this third synthesis is a synthesis of the first two: it is a "synthesis of diversity and its reproduction,"[66] or "of difference and its repetition."[67] There is an important caveat to this synthesis of recognition, though. In the Kantian system, this coordination of the first two syntheses as well as this selection was formerly regulated by the categories. But this option is not available to Deleuze's Nietzsche. As I pointed out in the previous chapter, Deleuze explicitly calls for "a genesis of the understanding *and* its categories" in *Nietzsche and Philosophy*.[68] Thus, Deleuze needs a way of negotiating the first two syntheses which is not based on rule- or concept-based recognition where those rules or concepts are given in advance. In the same way that common notions in Deleuze's Spinoza referred to our activity insofar as they presuppose an act of invention, this third synthesis points toward the creation of a concept or a principle of selection—a rule which will ensure the synthesis of recognition. How this happens is clearest not in the theoretical register in *Nietzsche and Philosophy* but in the practical register.

Practically, Deleuze says, this third synthesis performs a "selection" of forces. The crucial point here is that this criteria needs to be invented. This is for several reasons, one of which is that reactivity is defined by our recourse to already-established patterns of behavior. This synthesis must, therefore, proceed by "active" "self-destruction" (or what I called in the previous chapter, "failure").[69] It must abandon the passive self and all its habits of acting and reacting. But in addition to this we might also notice that situations often arise in which we do not know how to respond, and in which we simply do not have readily available sensory-motor schemata to respond in a noncreative or habitual way (these moments form the transition between *Cinema I* and *Cinema II* and I will discuss them briefly in the next chapter).[70] As Levi Bryant argues in a compelling discussion of Deleuze's ethics, it is precisely in these situations that we turn to ethics. What is missing from traditional ethical philosophies, Bryant argues, is "the moment of the uncertain."[71]

[T]he moment of the ethical is precisely the moment of crisis. . . . The question of the ethical is not the question of how crisis can be ameliorated by recourse to preexisting principles for the simple reason that the ethical is encountered at just that moment where "principles" governing a composition no longer hold. Rather, the question of the ethical is that of how situations must be re-composed in response to this moment of crisis.[72]

What Deleuze shows in *Nietzsche and Philosophy* is that in these moments we need to *invent* a principle which is adequate to the situation. This is the function of the third synthesis, or the eternal return, in its practical aspect.

Deleuze even goes so far as to claim that the thought of the eternal return gives us a *rule*. "[A]s a thought, it gives the will a practical rule"—one "as rigorous as the Kantian one."[73] Nietzsche's formulation of the thought of the eternal return in its practical aspect goes like this: "If, in all that you will you begin by asking yourself: is it certain that I will do it an infinite number of times? This should be your most solid center of gravity."[74] Deleuze's commentary goes on to emphasize the way in which this thought would push us to the limit of our activity:

> One thing in the world disheartens Nietzsche: the little compensations, the little pleasures . . . . Everything can be done again the next day only on the condition that it be said the day before: tomorrow I will give it up—the whole ceremonial of the obsessed. And we are like those old women who permit themselves an excess only once, we act and think like them.[75]

This is one reading of the rule. We would not sneak hidden pleasures. And we should not wait until tomorrow to do what we needed to do today: we should either do it or forget about it. Even laziness and stupidity would be transformed: "Laziness, stupidity, baseness, cowardice or spitefulness that would will its own eternal return would no longer be the same laziness, stupidity, etc."[76]

But Deleuze immediately reformulates Nietzsche to make him sound more Kantian: "*whatever you will, will it in such a way that you also will its eternal return*,"[77] and this formulation requires that we read this in relation to Kant's categorical imperative. When we do, a major difference appears. The best way to approach this is to notice where the locus of repetition lies in each principle. In the Kantian formulation, it lies in the action. Lying in any situation, even philanthropic lying, is categorically wrong. In the eternal return (in its "cosmological" aspect), what is repeated is not the action, but rather what we might call "the situation or the state of affairs." It is from this particular, even singular, configuration of events that an action must be selected (in its practical aspect). As Deleuze puts it in *The Logic of Sense*, the ethical question is how we might become adequate not to a rational law or a kingdom of ends, but to the event.[78] If the will to power for Deleuze is a plastic and genetic principle which changes and molds itself according to the forces which it determines and which determine it—a principle which is, therefore, adequate not to the conditions of possible experience but to the exigencies of real experience—then the thought of the eternal return is the principle which is adequate to the will to power's corporeal plasticity at the level of thought. It molds itself to the requirements of the situation.

Like Deleuze's Ideas, it is not the thought of a possible action, but of a singular action in a determinate situation. In this moment, thinking becomes properly active, and its activity is manifested in a fundamental creativity. While Deleuze does not emphasize this, we might notice that thought becomes free here in two senses. It is free, first of all, in the break it makes from passivity through the process of active self-destruction. It is no longer subject to the play of forces at the level of the body.[79] It is free second of all in the sense that thought here invents its own law. It becomes autonomous. This is what Deleuze does emphasize. The thought of the eternal return "makes willing a creation,"[80] and transforms our will into an "*artistic* will" which fully realizes its activity through a process of "selection, correction, redoubling, and affirmation" in which it formulates a "practical rule."[81] When Deleuze says that the thought of the eternal return opens up the "possibility of transmutation as a new way of feeling, thinking, and above all being"[82] then, we need to understand this in two ways. The "possibility of transmutation" is secured by our freedom from passivity; the new ways of feeling which are invented in this rupture are the productions of thought as a creative faculty which gives itself its own law.

This represents a new understanding of thought as *essentially creative*, and it is from this point of view that we can see the distance between Spinozan rationality and Deleuzian virtuality. In *Nietzsche and Philosophy*, Deleuze makes this point by pitting Nietzsche against Kant, but the distinction he draws between "thought" and "reason" works equally well for measuring his distance from Spinoza (especially considering the very Kantian spin Deleuze put on his discussion of reason in Spinoza).

The basic idea here is that the highest form of thought is embodied in neither calculation nor legislation but in creation: "to think is to create."[83] Deleuze draws the distinction between creative thought and legislating reason from the point of view of their relation to "life" (which at this point in the book characterizes the reciprocal relationship between the will to power and the forces it gathers together):

> Rational knowledge sets the same limits to life as reasonable life sets to thought; life is subject to knowledge and at the same time thought is subject to life. Reason sometimes dissuades and

sometimes forbids us to cross certain limits: because it is useless (knowledge is there to predict), because it would be evil (life is there to be virtuous), because it is impossible (there is nothing to see or think behind the truth).[84]

This characterization of reason depends on the close relation between thought and life. When thought is rational, life gets caught up in its grids; when life is rational (this seems to mean that life focuses exclusively on its preservation and out of fear restricts itself only to "scientifically observable reactions"[85]), so is thought. Rationality is like a disease which affects both thought and life. Thought as reason predicts outcomes, determines the good, and thinks the true. Life acts accordingly and becomes rational life, striving to persevere not in pursuit of joy but in a flight from death. The problem with this definition of knowledge is less that it is factually wrong, but that it is reactive. In language which intentionally alludes to the Kantian Copernican revolution (Kant proposes the idea of a "necessary submission of the object to the 'finite' subject: to us, the legislators, in our very finitude"[86]) Deleuze explains that, "this knowledge that measures, limits and moulds life is itself entirely modeled on reactive life."[87]

Nietzsche gives thought a new determination according to Deleuze. He frees it from its subjection "to reason and all that reason expresses."[88] Does this not give thought "another sense," Deleuze asks, making it a "thought that would go to the limit of what life can do"?

> Life would be the active force of thought, but thought would be the affirmative power of life. Both would go in the same direction, carrying each other along, smashing restrictions, matching each other step for step, in a burst of unparalleled creativity. Thinking would then mean *discovering, inventing, new possibilities of life*.[89]

The faculty of thought indeed takes on an entirely new sense here. It is no longer constrained by reason or by rational life, and life is no longer bound by the ideals of the good, the true, and the useful. The Spinozan ideal of a rational organization of life no longer holds and our power of action is not reason. (But neither does the Bergsonian insistence on the utility of thought hold—the idea that all thoughts, even the most general, are ultimately subject to the "fundamental law of life which is a law of action"—which I will discuss in the next chapter).[90] Thought, in Deleuze's Nietzsche, breaks from the category of rationality (as well as that of utility). In smashing all restrictions, it represents the permanent crisis recognition and its rule-bound unity. Thought becomes creative and life opens on to new possibilities. "There is creation, properly speaking, only insofar as we make use of excess in order to invent new forms of life."[91]

Notice, however, that Deleuze does not dispute the distinctly Spinozan intimacy of thinking and life. This does not change in the new formulation of the faculty of thought. The Spinozan view according to which the "different kinds of knowledge are also different ways of living, different modes of existing" because they are "different configurations of life" seems to structure Deleuze's thinking here as well. Indeed, Deleuze's typology in *Nietzsche and Philosophy*—the guilty man, the ascetic man, the man who cannot have done with anything, and so on—is based on different configurations of life: each type is discovered by inquiring into "the real forces that *form* thought."[92] What has changed between Spinoza and Nietzsche is not the close connection between thought and life but the definition of "thought" itself. It is no longer a *ratio* reinforcing reactive, sensory-motor forces, but an unbounded creativity from which active affections flow. When the subject reaches this essence or vocation and becomes active, it no longer organizes its affections rationally. It takes advantage of its excess to create new possibilities for life or new configurations of the body. The name for the type of thinker, who affirms life, carrying thought and life toward new possibilities, is "the artist."

Joy and perfection

My general argument in this chapter is that *Nietzsche and Philosophy* and *Expressionism in Philosophy* presented a genetic picture of the subject which is sufficiently similar to Deleuze's picture of the subject in *Difference and Repetition* to allow us to begin to develop some general propositions pertaining to Deleuze's ethics. The central concept in both of these texts is that of joy. In both texts, Deleuze takes issue with the "moral" categories of Good and Evil, replacing them with the "ethical" categories of the good and the bad.[93] The good is what increases my power of action and thus produces joyful affections; the bad is what diminishes my power and causes sad passions. The good, we might say, is known quite simply by pleasure or joy. Joy is not good in and of itself, however; and Deleuze's ethics do not devolve here into a calculus of quantities of pleasure. And this is not only because pleasure is merely the effect of an increase in activity which is itself the real good. As Deleuze says, this is merely a "preliminary" way of understanding it.[94] Pleasure and activity are good insofar as they allow me to attain not any activity, but my power of activity, my essence, or my virtuality. They are good insofar as they advance "a development, a formative process, a culture" and thus contribute to my flourishing and perfection. The end of this process is that point at which "our power of action has so increased that it becomes capable of producing affections that are themselves active"—but it is rare that we achieve this.[95] In the meantime, we call those encounters "good" which cultivate our faculties and draw us nearer to our power of action.[96]

In an important essay, Pierre Macherey argued that Deleuze "distorts" Spinoza in three ways: he amplifies the theme of expression, he artificially separates quality and quantity, and he overemphasizes, and potentially completely invents, the role of the joyful passions. This latter charge is the most important for this discussion, and it is something I took care to emphasize above: there is no development without pleasure. It is what gives birth to the imagination, to the understanding and to reason. At every step of the genesis, joy is the operative principle. Macherey argues, however, that in Spinzoa, there is no such thing as a joyful passion. All passions are, by definition, sad. There are ways to counter Macherey's reading[97]—and, as he points out, this is a very difficult aspect of Spinoza's thought—and defend Deleuze's reading. But it is better, I think, to affirm it (and not just because Macherey is such a formidable reader of Spinoza). This emphasis on joy *is* a "constructive device," "the mark of an encounter" that defines Deleuze's "experiment" in philosophical commentary.[98] It is also something we find in many of Deleuze's other texts. One of the ways in which Deleuze develops the dynamic genesis in *Difference and Repetition* and *The Logic of Sense* is in the language of psychoanalytic drives. In order for the subject to evolve, it is necessary that the drive be satisfied.[99]

My argument here is that Deleuze's ethics are perfectionist in the sense that they lead up to a certain "focal point" or "point of transmutation." By making that defining characteristic not rationality, but creativity or the production of the new, Deleuze puts us in touch with an essence that is not yet in existence, or rather an essence which is open and which creates thoughts that fold back on the surrounding architecture of the subject, giving it new shapes, possibilities, and desires. In other words, he does not give us an account of the perfect. Humans, as he put it in the title of his review of Foucault's *Order of Things*, have a "dubious existence." And this view is not solely the result of the book under review. Many of Deleuze's early essays turn around the possibility that the essence of humanity is something other than humanity. As he puts it in *Instincts et institutions*, "The human is an animal decimating its species."[100] In *Nietzsche and Philosophy*, this takes on perhaps the clearest expression in the final pages where Deleuze emphasizes that the thought of the eternal return does not simply bypass reactivity, it transcends our very species-being as such. When we become fully creative, we break with the properly human.[101] Deleuze thus categorically rejects Heidegger's interpretation which "turns the Overman into the realization and even determination of the human essence" on the grounds that "The essence of man and of the world occupied by man is the becoming-reactive of all forces."[102] Humanity is merely the skin disease of the earth. The Overman overcomes man altogether. And this is what makes Deleuze's perfectionism paradoxical: the ethical brings us not into our perfection, but into something beyond it. "The aim of critique is not the ends of man or of reason but in the end the Overman, the overcome, overtaken man. The point of critique is not justification but a different way of feeling: another sensibility."[103] As Cavell puts it in his formulation of Emersonian perfectionism, what is at issue here is the "next self."[104] This next self, I've argued, is conditioned on the production of an artistic will.

4

Aesthetics

Art is the opposite of a 'disinterested' operation: it does not heal, calm, sublimate or pay off, it does not 'suspend' desire, instinct or will. On the contrary, art is a 'stimulant of the will to power', 'something that excites willing'.[1]

One way to approach Deleuze's aesthetics would be to amass the various statements Deleuze has made about art and generalize from them to some kind of general definition. Take these three, for example:

1. "Composition, composition is the sole definition of art."[2]
2. "The work of art" is "*a bloc of sensations, that is to say a compound of percepts and affects.*"[3]
3. "Can this becoming, this emergence [of a territory] be called Art? That would make the territory a result of art. The artist: the first person to set out a boundary stone, or to make a mark."[4]

Each of these statements individually yields provocative positions with respect to questions of the nature, function, and possibilities of art. But this approach runs into several immediate difficulties, the most important of which is that the context of these utterances is never clear. By "context," I do not just mean that the third statement is thinking the question of art in relation to animal life, while the first and second put "art" in relation to "science." I mean primarily that it is never clear how these statements relate to the ontological structures which lie at the foundation of Deleuze's central texts. Any attempt to get to the bottom of his aesthetics this way risks missing Deleuze's most basic approach to art. This view that I'm looking for *is* provided by Deleuze's book-length works on Proust, Francis Bacon, and film. We can discern a basic pattern in his approach to aesthetics in each of these texts which stretches all the back to the earliest.

The first of these, *Proust and Signs* (1964), develops an account of the signs populating Proust's work. There are three types of signs: signs of the world, signs of love, and signs of art. These signs are not drawn inductively from Proust's text. Deleuze did not survey the volumes and abstract the three main kinds of signs structuring the novel from a plurality of less interesting signs. Rather these signs constitute the structure of an *apprenticeship*—"a development, a formative process, a culture."[5] They are staged according to the various levels Marcel reaches in his education. He begins with the signs of the social world and learns to decipher the encoded conventions. He moves on to signs of love and learns to read the possible worlds hidden in the gestures of the lover. And finally, at the end, he learns to read the signs of art which express the singular essences of all signs. But the structure of this education is not accidental, and it would not have gone differently for Swann, for example. As Deleuze makes clear at the end of the 1964 text, Marcel's apprenticeship travels along a line of faculties. Each sign awakens and cultivates a new faculty. Far from being induced from a total and contingent set of signs gathered from across the *Search*, then, these signs are *deduced* from a necessary structure of subjectivity—one which corresponds to the dynamic genesis outlined in Chapter 2.

This referral of aesthetic questions to the unfolding of subjectivity is considerably more difficult to see in Deleuze's later text, *Francis Bacon* (1981), due to the text's organization, but this theory of subjectivity is still operative here, and the logic of sensation which Deleuze finds Bacon's *oeuvre* is stretched across the eight-stage structure described in Chapter 2: there is the plane of sensation from which we ascend, through three syntheses (the clinch, the couple, and the forced movement), to the diagram. Only from the diagram can we ascend, finally, to the figure, a living representation which is beyond all cliché.

The articulation of this subjectivity is obviously not the (or even *a*) central task of *Francis Bacon*, but the text remains deeply mysterious if we do not follow Deleuze's references back to his ontology. The most well developed of these endeavors, of course, is his two-volume work on film—*Cinema I* (1983) and *Cinema II* (1985)—and it is with these texts that this chapter is primarily concerned. The first and largest part of this chapter is a close reading of *Cinema I* and *Cinema II*. The primary goal of this is to show that these two books are built around the backbone of the ontology I described in Chapter 2. In the second part of the chapter, I argue that Deleuze's aesthetics replay Kant's on a new stage—the central modification being that the spectator and the artist both are necessarily *interested*. The consequence of this is that Deleuze's aesthetics are immediately ethical. At the core of Deleuze's ethics was the thinker who affirms life, carries thought and life toward new possibilities, and who Deleuze calls in a Nietzschean idiom, "the artist." Conversely, at the core of Deleuze's aesthetics, we rediscover the problem of ethics insofar as the vocation of the artist is the positive invention of new possibilities for life.

Cinema I and *Cinema II*

Alain Badiou, in his arguments about Deleuze's monotony, specifically singles out *Cinema I* and *Cinema II*: Deleuze "singularly analyzes work after work" with a "disconcerting erudition," but in the end, the impressive analysis of all these films ends in a kind of radical reduction— a "siphoning into the reservoir of concepts" that, from the very beginning of his work, Deleuze has linked together: namely, movement and time . . . .[6] In what follows, I want to push this argument considerably further. Badiou is certainly right in saying that the themes of time and movement here echo Deleuze's early works, and most obviously and directly to the themes of *chronos* and *aion* in *The Logic of Sense*. In the same way that *The Logic of Sense* moved from the primary order of movement to the secondary organization of sense in the empty form of time, the cinema books move from a plane of movement-images to a plane of time-images. But, Badiou's observation can be pushed into extreme detail. Each step in the works' progress replays the basic moments of subjectivity developed in Deleuze's earlier texts.

The body-hyphen

The best way to show this is to review Deleuze's "deduction" of subjectivity in *Cinema I*.[7] We know, on a first reading—or even simply from reading the table of contents—that cinema for Deleuze is a collection of signs and images, that particular films express certain of these images, and that of all the images, there are five central ones: movement-images, perception-images, affection-images, action-images, and time-images. We can even lay them out in a chart which illustrates the basic formal structure of *Cinema I*:

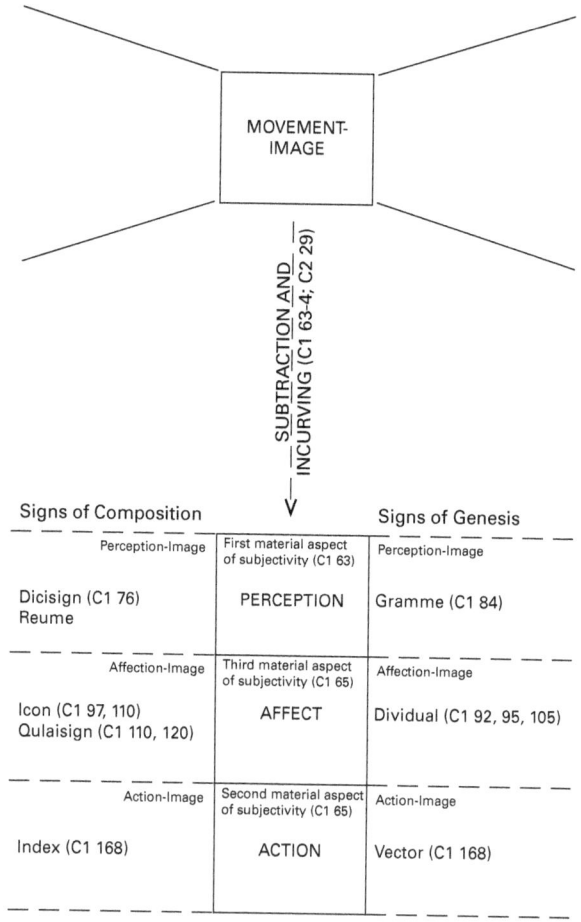

Schema of *Cinema I*

Like the signs of *Proust and Signs*, these images are not abstracted from the general set of images in the history of cinema. They are "deduced," and this deduction replays a familiar and perhaps, by now, monotonous pattern.

This is most clear if we look, for the last time, at the original position of *Cinema I* and *II*. Deleuze asks us to grant Bergson two concepts: a plane of immanence and an interval on that plane. The plane of immanence is the apparently unregulated interaction of matter (C1 61). It is a tumultuous world in which material elements, "images," act and react on one another in all their parts and facets to infinity.

> Let us call the set of what appears 'Image'. We cannot even say that one image acts on another or reacts to another. There is no moving body (*mobile*) which is distinct from executed movement. There is nothing moved which is distinct from the received movement. Every thing, that is to say every image, is indistinguishable from its actions and reactions: this is universal variation. Every image is 'merely a road by which pass, in every direction, the modifications propagated throughout the immensity of the universe'. *Every image acts on others and reacts to others, on 'all their facets at once' and 'by all their elements'.*[8]

Elsewhere in the text, Deleuze will say that the plane of immanence, or the "set of what appears," is a field of matter in flux. Here, however, the emphasis is entirely on the state of constant movement. The plane of immanence is not so much a field of pure material bodies, but the "universal *variation*" of bodies. Every body is merely a road across which movement travels to infinity. Whatever appears in this set is entirely dissolved in its affections and reactions. To be a body, as he put it in *Expressionism in Philosophy*, is to be "affected in a very great number of ways."[9]

The importance of perpetual movement in this characterization becomes clear in the second given of the deduction: the interval. The interval interrupts the immediate transformation of action into reaction by introducing a space of delay between two movements. Bergson calls this space of originary delay "the body." The body, he writes, is "a *place of passage* of the movements received and thrown back, a hyphen, a connecting link between the things which act upon me and the things upon which I act—the seat, in a word, of the sensory-motor phenomena" (MM 152). Both Deleuze and Bergson will emphasize that the body is part of the world—it is, "in this material world, that part of which we directly feel the flux" (MM 139), Bergson writes—but the overwhelming emphasis at this early stage seems to fall on its function as a hyphen. It is a "connecting link" between action and reaction.

To call this interval "the body" implies that it is an already constituted body and that it is not subject to a development. What Deleuze seems to have in mind here, however, is a larval and gaseous subjectivity:

> My body is an image, hence a set of actions and reactions. My eye, my brain, are images, parts of my body. . . . External images act on me, transmit movement to me, and I return movement: how could images be in my consciousness since I am myself image, that is, movement? And can I even, at this level, speak of 'ego', of eye, of brain and of body? Only for simple convenience; for nothing can yet be identified in this way. It is rather a gaseous state. Me, my body, are rather a set of molecules and atoms which are constantly renewed. Can I even speak of atoms? (C1 58)

Here we have the central components of the Bergsonian body: the body is an image; it participates directly in the flux of matter; it is a center of indetermination which allows me to select, organize, and transmit received movements. But it is just as clear that the body is not yet any kind of fully constituted body. It is an unconstituted, unindividuated, "gaseous" body. Depending on our taste for imagery, we could follow Deleuze in *The Logic of Sense* and say either that our body is dissolved in matter like a drop of wine in the ocean or that it is uncontrollably tossed about in a universal cesspool.[10] In either case, ocean or cesspool, it seems that Deleuze is saying simultaneously that our body is a part of this flux and that it is not yet our body: we can only call it "a body" for the sake of convenience because it not yet anything more than a hyphen which is "constantly renewed."

This emphasis on the body as a hyphen risks overemphasizing its connective capacity. At the same time this link connects, it also disconnects. It is a link which is also a pause or a delay, and it is this function which makes Deleuze's deduction possible. As Deleuze puts it, "By virtue of the interval" opened up by the body, we become capable of "delayed reactions which have time to *select* their elements, to *organize* them or to *integrate* them into a new movement . . ." (C1 62; my emphases). Selection, organization, and integration are the three basic functions of the body, and if we briefly outline the way they operate, it becomes immediately apparent that the structure of Deleuze's deduction more or less repeats the process of passive (or, we could say, sensory-motor) synthesis which characterized the dynamic genesis in Deleuze's other works and which I have described in the previous chapters.

It is not necessary to spend much time on the first half of this deduction—that which comprises the dynamic genesis or the system of the passive self—because Deleuze himself is exceedingly clear about how it works, and *Cinema I* as a whole is dedicated to developing its itinerary in detail. We can, therefore, keep this part of the exposition rather short and indicate the direction in which Deleuze is moving across *Cinema I*. Whereas images on the plane of immanence acted on and reacted to one another in all of their parts and facets in an infinite "communication,"[11] by virtue of the interval, the body interrupts communication and submits the relation of action and reaction to a form of mediation. The first thing that happens at this point is that the actions of other bodies on mine become "excitations" which my body "*perceivos*." Deleuze himself translates this moment into the Kantian idiom I have been using throughout this book. The perception-image is an "*apprehension* of the plane of immanence" (C1 62). The body "perceives" movement-images and "frames" them (C1 63). He says here that it "selects" images; in the language of *Difference and Repetition*, we could say that it "contracts" instants or "binds" intensities.

In the same way, the second moment of sensory-motor subjectivity—the affection-image or the interval's power of "organization"—becomes a synthesis of reproduction and recording. Whereas the perception-image selected movement images on the plane of immanence, the affection-image "absorbs" "external movements" (C1 62). It opens up a space of recording in which movements, possible actions, and past actions can all be recorded and retained for future use. If we wanted to put this in the language of Deleuze's earlier texts, we could say that the affection-images constitute a passive memory, or a "grid of disjunctions" in which the "data" of the first synthesis is "recorded" (AO 38).

The last moment of sensory-motor subjectivity—that of "reintegration" in the action-image—is the one with which I am primarily concerned here. It functions, as I will argue in the next section, as a synthesis of recognition, and its failure will propel us from the realm of the movement-image to that of the time-image (from the dynamic genesis to the static genesis; from intensity to virtuality; from life to thought; and so on). But before we follow that movement in detail, it is worth addressing an immediate problem.

From the perspective of this deduction and its Bergsonist vocabulary, it is difficult to understand what role *cinema* might play in all of this. There are two complimentary ways of understanding this (and I will suggest a third at the end of the chapter). On the one hand, Deleuze will constantly say things to the effect that this theory of images and their combinations "explains" cinema. What he provides us with is a well-grounded table of images which lets us classify what we see in actual films in the same way Linnaeus's table allowed him to classify what he saw in his plants.[12] On the basis of the strong similarities between this cinematic subject and the subject at the foundation of Deleuze's ontology, however, we might point out that if this table "explains" images, it is only insofar as it refers them back to a specifically Deleuzian architecture of the subject, and thus requires that we accept this account of subjectivity before Deleuze's taxonomy takes on any explanatory power. On the other hand, however, cinema also seems to have a revelatory function, and *it* can explain, in turn, these various stages in the progressive development of the body. As Paola Marrati puts it, cinema transforms itself in Deleuze's hands into an "instrument in service of revelation."[13] For Deleuze, Beckett can bring us all the way back to the "plane of matter and its cosmic eddying of movement-images" (C1 68). Vertov shows us "the *genetic element* of all possible perception" (83; original emphasis). Duras and Michael Snow reveal the genetic element of the affection-image (122). Kazan shows us the genetic element of the action-image (155). And Welles, among others, will open our eyes to the time-image.

This question of the relation between cinema and subjectivity is obviously more complex than this, and I will return to it below. But, by the end of *Cinema I*, we are only halfway through the deduction. It is necessary to understand how we open on to the virtual, or time in its pure state, and how, from there, we return to the body.

Recognition and its crises: From movement to time

The action-image is the third moment of the passive or sensory-motor subject. It is one of the most complex of all the images, but in its general structure, it is relatively straightforward: it involves a synthesis of perception and affection. "We enter into the realm of the action-image," Deleuze writes, when "qualities and powers are apprehended as actualized in states of things" (C1 123). By "qualities and powers," Deleuze is referring to the components of the affection-image. If these powers and qualities are "apprehended as actualized in states of things" in the action-image, this can only mean that affections are folded back onto states of things or perceptions. In the action-image, the affection-image is combined with the perception-image. This is the genetic definition of the action-image: "The pair of *object* and *emotion* thus appears in the action-image as its genetic sign" (158; my emphasis). In Bergson, this unity of a perception and memory is called "recognition."[14] Recognition, Bergson writes, is "the concrete process by which we grasp the past in the present" or the way we utilize a "past experience for a present action" (MM 90, 78). From this point of view, Deleuze remains thoroughly Bergsonian: the action-image is a synthesis of recognition—or to put this in words which will become increasingly important across the course of *Cinema II*, recognition constitutes an initial link between "man" and "world."

For Bergson, there are two types of recognition, involuntary and voluntary. The kind with which we are concerned in the action-image and its eventual crisis is only the first kind of recognition: sensory-motor or involuntary recognition. Involuntary recognition has several important characteristics. First, it is entirely pre-representational. It is, Bergson writes, an "instantaneous recognition, of which the body is capable by itself, without the help of any explicit memory-image. It consists in action and not in representation" (MM 93). Bergson will often say that in motor recognition, the past is not represented, but acted. Second, involuntary recognition is habitual, passive, and does not require the intervention of an active, conscious mind. It is composed of "motor mechanisms created by repetition." "Our whole life is passed among a limited number of objects," Bergson tells us,

> Each of them, as it is perceived, provokes on our part movements, at least nascent, whereby we adapt ourselves to it. These movements, as they recur, contrive a mechanism for themselves, grow into habit, and determine in us *attitudes* which automatically follow our perception of things. (MM 84; my emphasis)

Sensory-motor recognition, thus, remains on the plane of immanence, in the world of action and reaction. It never passes through representation or conscious activity. The "cosmic eddies" on the plane of immanence throw trillions of excitations our way, and our body passively adapts itself to them. It "contrives a mechanism" for coping with various excitations. And because all of this happens below the threshold of representation, our involuntary responses, or reactions, are not expressed in representations, but in bodily *attitudes* or *postures* (MM 81–2).

There are important systematic differences between Deleuze and Bergson which emerge at this point. Both Deleuze and Bergson (unlike Kant) make the *failure* of recognition an integral part of their philosophy, but Deleuze will take this considerably further than Bergson. In *Matter and Memory*, there is indeed something like a crisis in the action-image: recognition fails repeatedly. In an unfamiliar situation, for example, I might not be able to find a habitual response in my affective memory. In such a situation, Bergson says, I have to pay attention and penetrate more deeply into the object. And, further, I have to mobilize active memory-images which will allow me to actively respond to received movements. The whole dialectic between body and world here moves from the pre-representational world of motor memory to the representational world of attentive perception and memory-images. But this hardly constitutes a *crisis*. It is simply a fact of life. In fact, it seems that memory likes it. Cut off from the real, and powerless to realize itself by itself, memory exerts a constant pressure on the body, waiting for a chance to slip back into the real (MM 152–3).

Always inhibited by the practical and useful consciousness of the present moment, that is to say, by the sensori-motor equilibrium of a nervous system connecting perception with action, this memory merely awaits the occurrence of a rift between the actual impression and its corresponding movement to slip in its images. (95)

Memory cannot realize itself of its own accord, and when a rift—a crisis in the action-image—occurs, memory "slips in" to the body. What I want to emphasize here is that this active or voluntary recognition appears as a backup plan. In the event that sensory-motor recognition fails, intellectual recognition slips in and fills the gap. It gives the body what it needs to determine an action, and, in exchange, "memory borrows" from the body "the warmth which gives it life" (153). In other words, in Bergson, the man-world link is immediately restored. The only cases when the link is not restored are those in which it is quite literally severed: "cerebral lesions" or "diseases of the faculty of recognition" (107–8).

Deleuze, however, makes this crisis of recognition an integral part of nondiseased subjectivity in general. He calls it the crisis in the action-image, and it is what propels us into the dimension of the time-image. At the end of *Cinema I*, we remain entirely within the context of the failure of involuntary recognition, but this is where *Cinema II* begins. "This is the first aspect of the new cinema: the break in the sensory-motor link (action-image), and more profoundly in the link between man and the world (great organic composition)" (C2 173). This link is not restored for Deleuze by the intervention of an active-recognition or by memory-images which take advantage of the rift to "slip in." Over the course of the early chapters of *Cinema II*, Deleuze progressively takes away the prospects of a voluntary recognition filling this gap. His discussion of German expressionism is particularly important in this regard. In expressionist and certain surrealist films, a "character finds himself prey to visual and sound sensations" just as the characters of Antonioni and Rossellini had when their *involuntary* recognition failed. With the expressionists and surrealists, however, "these actual sensations and perceptions *are as cut off from memory-based recognition as they are from motor recognition*" (55; my emphasis). In other words, there is no memory hovering behind perception to come to its rescue for Deleuze. In the failure of recognition we remain face to face with images without any habitual interpretation of them. What we finally reach in the early Welles is something beyond all recognition: "as soon as we reach the sheets of past it is as if we were carried away by the undulations of a great wave, time gets out of joint, and we enter into temporality as a state of *permanent crisis*" (112; original emphasis). The crisis in recognition throws us into time itself, but it gives us time as a permanent crisis of recognition.

This systematic difference between Bergson and Deleuze has deep roots in Deleuze's earlier philosophy. In the *Logic of Sense*, he even invented a principle for it: "counter-actualization." The virtual—or "sense"—does not simply break from sensory-motor subjectivity, it actively maintains its hard-won distance from the universal cesspool of corporeal depths through counteractualization. If "actualization" is the name for the process by which thought (and its Ideas) returns to matter and individuates it, counteractualization is the process by which thought holds the ocean of unindividuated materiality at a distance (LS 168; cf. WP 160). The aleatory point, or the "non-actualizable part of the event," counteractualizes corporeal depths and allows thought to go about its work of forming Ideas with minimal distraction.

Just as the virtual actively maintains its autonomy from corporeality, the time-image has to remain radically independent of the plane of immanence.[15] Beyond sonsigns and opsigns, crystal images and dream images, cinema reveals time as the "permanent crisis" of recognition, and in this crisis, it discovers both thought's essence—the aleatory point—and its own essence (C2 168).

Becoming active

Deleuze's texts return to this scene of failure again and again. In the previous chapter, it constituted what Levi Bryant called "the moment of the ethical" or the "moment of crisis" at which thought is propelled to become, adequate to life and, conversely, life to thought. It is the moment in *Difference and Repetition* and *The Logic of Sense* at which the faculty of thought becomes properly creative and draws on the power of the aleatory point to think Ideas. This is, indeed, what

AESTHETICS

happens here. In the failure of recognition, we discover our power of activity or creativity. When the turn to voluntary recognition in a representational memory becomes not only "pointless," but also "impossible," and when cinema, in the hands of Resnais and Artaud, shows "time as perpetual crisis," a pure "sheet of transformation," or a "network of non-localizable relations" which subtends all sheets of the past and which holds them together (123), we discover, at the heart of this failure, the "aleatory point" (175). This aleatory point is characterized here in terms nearly identical to those used in Deleuze's other texts. It is "an always extrinsic point of thought" (175), a "point of the outside" (176) which transforms thought from a "regime of localizable relations, actual linkages, legal causal and logical connections" (127) into an infinite overlapping of perspectives defined by relationships which make no immediate sense and by connections which have no apparent relation to the demands of action or life (129–30). It is through its manipulation of this creative point, Deleuze says, that cinema discovers its "vocation." The filmmaker who embodies the "artistic will" (C2 141; NP 103) here is Welles. He takes control of the new from its birth and uses it to create new ways of seeing, feeling, and acting; Welles is "always increasing the power to live, always opening new possibilities" (C2 141).

Up until this point, *Cinema I* and *II* are more or less clear and explicit about what they are doing and the ways in which they are replaying the conceptual structures of Deleuze's earlier texts. But at this point in *Cinema II*, the formal clarity with which Deleuze distinguished between perception, affection, and action is almost completely absent. In particular, at this juncture, any reader of Bergson, and especially of Deleuze's Bergson, has to be wondering what happened to the theory of actualization. This is an especially significant omission given the position of the Deleuzian subject at this point in its formation: it has emerged from a plane of immanence, attained its power of activity but now remains cut off from the world. If Deleuze's thought were only the pursuit of an unbounded creativity, and if the sole end of its method were to leave us face to face with Ozu's vase in semimystical experience of time, it would be enough to stop here. But, obviously, Deleuze does not stop here in any of his works. Once the virtual is discovered, the task is to show how its Ideas are actualized. In other words, the task is to show how Ideas individuate and thereby *shape* the world. How do you get from a state of permanent crisis back to the sphere of activity? Actualization is the Bergsonist answer to this question, but this answer does not, at first sight, seem to play a role in *Cinema II*. There are, however, two ways in which the theory of actualization appears in *Cinema II*. The first and most obvious place in which we find a theory of actualization, is in the thematics of "faith" or "belief." The link between man and world was broken in the failure of recognition. What we need from cinema, Deleuze says, is the restoration of that link.

> Man is in the world as if in a pure optical and sound situation. The reaction of which man has been dispossessed can be replaced only by belief. Only belief in the world can reconnect man to what he sees and hears. (C2 172)

It is not exactly clear how this would happen though. This theme of belief is essentially Humean, and Deleuze's treatment of faith here relates back to his 1953 reading of Hume. There, Deleuze identifies causal relationships as those which restore our faith in the world ("The privilege that causality enjoys is that it alone can make us affirm existence and make us believe."[16]) But there is no mention of Hume here, and the entire emphasis at this point in the text is on noncausal and a-logical connections. Thus, while "faith" or "belief" is the answer to our question, Deleuze says very little about *how* the concept of faith might restore the link between man and the world or embody a process of actualization.

At one point, Deleuze makes the provocative claim that this restoration might be possible through "the power of the genesis of postures" (200). Discussing the films of Philippe Garrel, Deleuze writes:

> This may be the first case of a cinema of constitution, one which is truly constitutive: constituting bodies, and in this way restoring our belief in the world, restoring our reason. . . (C2 200–1)

This passage identifies what is at stake in the question of faith. In *Cinema I*, the body was a gaseous body. It was passive and subject to the chaotic affections communicated to it across the plane of immanence. Here, at the end of *Cinema II*, Deleuze attributes to the concept of faith the possibility of transforming the gaseous body into an individuated body through the genesis of postures. But again, "faith" only seems to name the problem. In order to see how Deleuze works through this, we have to turn to the second way in which a theory of actualization appears in this text.

The second place in which we can see the theory of actualization return is in a set of coordinated allusions to Bergson. While the word "actualization" seems to be missing here, its attendant concepts are not. In the absence of a fifth commentary on Bergson, then, it is worth briefly reviewing the concept of actualization as Deleuze described it in *Bergsonism*. Recall that for Bergson, our recollections are not representations, but express themselves in bodily *attitudes* or *postures* (MM 81–2). In order for recollections and memory-images to pass into "movements" or actions and thus become actual, Bergson says that the body must first take on "a certain attitude into which recollections will come to insert themselves" (MM 99). (This works for Bergson in the other direction as well: certain postures can "call back [their] memory-image" (99, cf. 130)). Deleuze systematized Bergson's comments in his own account of actualization in *Bergsonism*. There are four aspects of actualization, Deleuze explains: translation, rotation, dynamic movement, and mechanical movement:

> translation and rotation, which form the properly psychic moments; dynamic movement, the attitude of the body that is necessary to the stable equilibrium of the preceding two determinations; and finally, mechanical movement, the motor scheme that represents the final stage of actualization. (BG 70)

It is these last two stages that are at issue here: the dynamic attitude of the body and its mechanical movement. To actualize a memory-image, the body must assume the correct posture or attitude, and it is only after that posture is assumed that memory will be able to re-enter the plane of immanence in the form of a reaction or a mechanical movement.

This plays out in the final chapters of *Cinema II* in the following way. Faith in the world, we find out, can only be restored by a "problematic, aleatory, and yet non-arbitrary point: grace or chance" (C2 175).[17] This point "alone is capable of restoring the world and the ego to us" (177, cf. 181). While it is initially Welles who takes on the role of the artist, it is later Godard. Godard discovers a "new synthesis" (184) which involves two innovations. The first replaces montage with "mixing" (179)—which Deleuze describes as the progressive determination of "differential relations" in the image (179); and second, he creates a table of categories or genres—"categories of problems" (186)—which regulate the mixing of images, arranging them in ordered series (184). In other words, what we see here in a disconnected way is the production of what Deleuze called "Ideas" in his earlier texts.

This is when the moment of actualization appears. Categories are then applied to the body. Although Deleuze likens these categories to the Aristotelian categories, it is clear from the start that they are not at all general concepts. They are "categories of life" (189). And insofar as the attitudes of the body are organized in the right way (this is the theory of gesture (192–3)), these categories can be said to "put time into the body, as well as thought into life" (192). Through this process, we "*restore* images to the attitudes and postures of the body" (193; my emphasis).

In its most abstract form, then, when we follow the movement from thought back to the body, we get: (1) an aleatory point which (2) produces categories that regulate the connection between images, but which can only do so by (3) becoming integrated in the mechanisms of the body. As Deleuze says, these categories "put time into the body, as well as thought into life" (C2 192); they "restore images to the attitudes and postures of the body" (193). In other words, they *actualize* the categories of life.

The theory of the body in the final chapters of *Cinema II* thus completes the deduction of subjectivity. After a detour through the virtual, the believing subject re-enters the plane of immanence and restores images to the attitudes and postures of the body, and, ultimately to mechanical movement. This is why believing in the world is ultimately believing in the body ("What is certain is that believing is no longer believing in another world, or in a transformed world. It is only, it is simply believing in the body" (C2 172)). The itinerary of *Cinema II* does not end, then, with the time-image or its varieties. The time-image represents (what we could call in a Spinzoist idiom) our essence, but it is essential to take control of the new from its

By putting these two sets of passages together, Deleuze answers Kant's question. The soul is a constitutive principle. It is not a psychological unity of the faculties, but a "suprasensible unity of all the faculties." And this unity is not static, but dynamic. It is a "*living unity.*"[75] It "vitalizes" and "gives life."[76] In other words, over the course of the first two books of the Critique, the mind has moved from a psychological and potentially animal faculty to a supersensible genetic element in which a genuinely genetic principle awakens our faculties from their "primeval state."

From Kant to Deleuze

Whether or not this is a persuasive reading of Kant (I think it is, but it would require substantial development), it gives us a final perspective on what it means to take up the Kantian initiative and to replay on a new stage. We seem to encounter in *The Critique of Judgment* exactly what Deleuze had been searching for in *The Critique of Pure Reason*. Recall that among Deleuze's criticisms of Kant were the claims that the critical philosophy (a) lacked a properly genetic principle and that it (b) subjected life to thought. These claims might be accurate with respect to the first Critique, but not with respect to Deleuze's reading of the third. Kant, on Deleuze's reading, "discovers" a genetic principle—the soul. And what's more, the *Critique of Judgment*, discovers, again on Deleuze's reading, an approach to life which *does not* subject it to thought. Deleuze is quite explicit about this:

> All legislation implies objects on which it is exercised and which are subject to it. Now, aesthetic judgment is not only always particular, of the type 'this rose is beautiful'. . . . More importantly, it does not even legislate over its singular object, since it remains completely indifferent to its existence.[77]

We seem incredibly close here to that productive principle Deleuze was looking for in *Nietzsche and Philosophy*: a principle which takes root in the detail of real experience, "an essentially *plastic* principle that is no wider than what it conditions, that changes itself with the conditioned and determines itself in each case along with what it birth and bring those relations back into the sphere of action through a process of actualization or belief.[18]

Cinema, subjectivity, and life

My central aim in the preceding section was to show that the theory of subjectivity around which the cinema books are structured is not exactly Bergsonian—or that it is so only to the extent that the structure of subjectivity underlying all of Deleuze's texts is Bergsonian. The conceptual backbone of *Cinema I* and *Cinema II* is firmly based on the theory of subjectivity developed in texts like *Difference and Repetition* and *The Logic of Sense*. This structural monotony does not carry over only to questions of movement and time or *chronos* and *aion*. It works its way into the very details of the passage from *chronos* to *aion* and back again. We ascend from movement to time by means of an apprehension, a reproduction and a failure of recognition. We return to an individuated matter by virtue of an actualization which puts the forms of time, Ideas, back into the body.

How are we to understand the presence of this subjectivity at the heart of Deleuze's major texts on art? This question has multiple senses. I have already argued above, for example, that subjectivity "explains" cinema at the same time that cinema reveals the structures of subjectivity. But we might also ask whether this subjectivity belongs to the artist or whether it belongs to the spectator? *Francis Bacon* would seem to decide the matter in favor of the former. By following Bacon's battle with the cliché and his construction of the diagram, Deleuze seems to be explaining the creative process and thus articulating the aesthetics of creation he called for in *Nietzsche and Philosophy*.[19] But in *Cinema I*, the question is answered in the other direction. It seems to be the spectator who is accosted by images (if the images on the plane of immanence have anything to do with the images on a screen[20]): cinema's images both organize and are organized by the brain's screen. *Proust and Signs*, though, presents a third option. The subject in question is neither the artist nor the spectator, but a fictional character. In other words, this question seems to be a false one. If the theory of subjectivity which Deleuze outlined in his formative texts is really ontological in scope, its structures must be general enough to apply to creators, spectators, and imagined subjects which strike us as plausible constructions (though, obviously, the processes and emphases will be different depending on which point of view we adopt).

The best way to understand this relationship between aesthetics and the structures of subjectivity is to see it as a flattening and pluralization of Kant's aesthetics. In the same way Deleuze's ontology reconfigured the *Critique of Pure Reason*, and in the same way his ethics inverted the moral law of the *Critique of Practical Reason*, Deleuze's aesthetics significantly rework the basic concepts of the *Critique of Judgment*. Because Deleuze's reading of the *Critique of Judgment* ties together his reading of the other two Critiques—Deleuze claimed that it revealed the hidden ground of the first two[21]—I spend considerably more time on it here.

Life, pleasure, and pain

A passage at the beginning of the *Critique of Judgment* sets the stage on which Deleuze's reworking is played out. Kant tells us that whereas the scientific judgments of the *Critique of Pure Reason* related representations to an object, aesthetic judgments relate representations to the subject or to its "feeling of life":

> Here the representation is related entirely to the subject, indeed to its feeling of life, under the name of the feeling of pleasure or displeasure, which grounds an entirely special faculty for discriminating and judging that contributes nothing to cognition but only holds the given representation in the subject up to the entire faculty of representation, of which the mind [*Gemüt*] becomes conscious in the feeling of its state.[22]

The dynamics of aesthetic judgment outlined in this passage provide the basic structure of the first two books of Kant's *Critique*. When we relate a representation to our feeling of life, or to our "entire faculty of representation," we become conscious of our "state." This state is capable of two general modifications: pleasure or pain. If the representation produces pleasure, we can say that it is beautiful (provided that the judgment is also disinterested, universal, purposive, and necessary); if the representation initially produces pain and then an "all the more powerful outpouring of pleasure," we can say it is sublime (provided, again, that the judgment is disinterested, universal, purposive, and necessary).[23]

Deleuze follows Kant in this initial gesture of referring representations to life. Images, Deleuze writes in *Francis Bacon*, bear "directly on the nervous system."[24] In *Cinema I* and *II*, images establish themselves in the interval between perception and action. Their structures represent ways of seeing (perception-image), feeling (affection-image), acting (action-image), and thinking (time-image). But at the same time, Deleuze's procedure leads to substantially different results: his aesthetics do not turn on the possibility of legitimately uttering "this is beautiful" or "this is sublime;" they turn rather on the possibility of understanding art as communicating ways of seeing, feeling, acting, and thinking. The reason for this divergence is grounded in a different conception of the foundations of aesthetic judgment.

This becomes clear—although not immediately—if we pursue the question of what Kant means by "life" in the passage above. Kant immediately refers the concept of life to our "feeling of pleasure or displeasure." Pleasure and displeasure are not easy to define, and Kant's most persistent position is that they cannot be explained in themselves. Pleasure and pain designate effects. The best we can do is take note of those effects so that we can "make them more cognizable in practice."[25] But Kant continually changed the way he talked about these effects and occasionally ventured explanations for them. In these alterations, we can hear important resonances with Deleuze's Spinoza and Deleuze's Nietzsche, and therefore with the dynamics which I argued in Chapter 3 were at the foundation of Deleuze's ethics.

In the *Anthropology*, for example, Kant characterizes pleasure as the desire to prolong an agreeable encounter. Whatever "urges me to *leave* my state (to go out of it) is *disagreeable* to me—it causes me pain; just as what drives me to *maintain* my state (to remain in it) is *agreeable* to me, I enjoy it."[26] This was the mechanism which led, in *Expressionism in Philosophy*, to the genesis of the imagination—the genesis of that faculty capable of maintaining the presence of an object even when the object itself was absent. As Deleuze writes there, "Insofar as the feeling of joy increases our power of action, it determines us to desire, imagine, do, all we can in order to preserve this joy itself and the object that procures it for us."[27] This act of preservation, the maintenance of a state by even artificial means, was how the imagination began to take shape in *Expressionism*. The next step in the genesis of the Spinozist subject, the understanding, provided a perspective on the first. We learn through common notions that those objects are pleasurable which agree with our nature.[28] So too, for Kant. In the *Critique of Practical Reason*, for example, he writes that "*Pleasure* is the idea of the agreement of an object or action with the *subjective* conditions of life."[29] What gives me pleasure is that which agrees with me.

Another way Kant talks about pleasure and pain resonates with Deleuze's Nietzsche. Pleasure is a "promotion" of our "powers of life" and pain is an "inhibition" of our powers. Thus, Kant writes, "What promotes our life, i.e., what brings our activity into play, as it were, pleases."[30] As Kant puts it in the *Anthropology*, pleasure is a "promotion of the vital force:"[31] "Enjoyment is the feeling of the promotion of life; pain is that of a hindrance of life."[32] For Deleuze's Nietzsche, an active force is one which promotes our power of life and pushes us to the limit of what we can do. A reactive force is a hindrance of our power of life and separates us from what we can do. The first causes joy; the second, sadness. While there are certainly important differences between Kant and Deleuze's Nietzsche, it is nevertheless the case that what Kant calls the *feeling of life* has important resonances with that field in which active and reactive forces encounter one another in the synthesis of the will to power. The fact that the will to power functions for Deleuze as a principle of synthesis which can replace the Kantian principle only heightens the stakes of these resonances insofar as it suggests that the genetic principle which Deleuze claimed to find in Nietzsche, and which supposedly rescued the Kantian concept of synthesis from the danger in which Kant had placed it, was already present in a more or less straightforward reading of Kant.

At this point, however, the similarities between Deleuze and Kant progressively diminish. We might begin by noticing that the first book of the *Critique of Judgment*, "The Analytic of the Beautiful," is devoted to developing a specifically aesthetic form of pleasure which draws on, but differs from, these earlier accounts of pleasure. I will return to this below, but we can say for now that our pleasure in the beautiful is engendered by the harmonious play of the imagination and the understanding, the two faculties operative in judgments of taste.[33] The beautiful work of art simultaneously liberates my imagination and, by virtue of its form, gives my understanding something to hold onto. The pleasure which follows from the judgment of taste, then, is neither a sensible pleasure, a moral pleasure, nor an intellectual pleasure. It is simply a pleasure I experience in the freedom and animation of my faculties.[34] It is a "*pleasure in the harmony of the faculties of cognition.*"[35] This pleasure has the same coordinates as the other forms of pleasure: it promotes our activity through the "animation of both faculties (the imagination and the understanding);"[36] both are "enlivened through mutual agreement."[37] And the effect of this promotion is that we strive to "*maintain*" our state.[38] We "**linger**" over the consideration of the beautiful."[39] But the pleasure here is related specifically to the "animation of [the subject's] cognitive powers."[40] What I feel in the judgment of the beautiful is my mind in a state of animation.[41] And thus the concept of life, the feeling of pleasure and displeasure, is linked to an equally problematic concept in Kant: that of the *Gemüt* or the mind in general.

The mind

It is with respect to the interpretation of this concept, the *Gemüt*, that the distance between Deleuze and Kant begins to sharpen. The "mind," for Kant, is that element in which all of our faculties are contained;[42] as Foucault put it, the mind is "organized by and armed with the faculties that divide up its domain."[43] Deleuze's reading of the third Critique in *Kant's Critical Philosophy* and in "The Idea of Genesis in Kant's Esthetics" is arguably a study of the destiny of this concept across *The Critique of Judgment*. With each step Kant takes, Deleuze suggests, the concept of the mind takes on renewed importance for transcendental philosophy until it becomes identified with the genetic point from which we can derive not only the *Critique of Judgment*, but also the entire critical project (I obviously leave this last claim to Deleuze). The best way to see this is to follow Deleuze's reading of the first two books of the *Critique of Judgment*: the "Analytic of the Beautiful" and the Analytic of the Sublime." The "Analytic of the Beautiful" opens with the passage I quoted above. Here Kant says that "in the feeling of its state" the "mind [*Gemüt*] becomes conscious" of the entire faculty of representation. Later in the *Critique*, Kant significantly reformulates this concept of the *Gemüt* in a long sentence which seems to assert a powerful link between mind and body. The sentence begins with a quiet criticism of Edmund Burke's claim that "The human mind is often, and . . . for the most part, in a state neither of pain nor pleasure, which I call a state of indifference."[44] Kant rejects this claim. "It cannot be denied," he writes, that all of our representations, whether sensible or intellectual, "can nevertheless subjectively be associated with gratification or pain, however unnoticeable either might be (because they all affect the feeling of life, and none of them, insofar as it is a modification of the subject, can be indifferent) . . . ."[45] All of our representations, everything we think, affect our feeling of life, and our power of life is subject to ceaseless modification, oscillating between pleasure and pain. We are never indifferent; we are only more or less unconscious of our difference.[46] Either as a consequence of this or just as a parallel insight, Kant finishes this sentence by adding that it also cannot be denied that

> . . . as Epicurus maintained, **gratification** and **pain** are always ultimately corporeal, whether they originate from the imagination of even from representations of the understanding: because life without the feeling of the corporeal organ is merely consciousness of one's existence, but not a feeling of well- or ill-being, i.e., the promotion or inhibition of the powers of life; because the mind (*Gemüt*) for itself is entirely life (the principle of life itself), and hindrances or promotions must be sought outside it, though in the human being himself, hence in combination with his body.[47]

These relations between mind, life, and feeling are complex, and are a subject of debate in Kant scholarship.[48] Life, here, is clearly an attribute of the mind. The mind (*Gemüt*) *is* life—the principle of life itself. But in itself it is simply consciousness of its existence.[49] It is life without the feeling of life. Our *feeling* of life, gratification or pain,

Kant asserts, is always ultimately corporeal.[50] The body thus seems to be the way the mind feels itself and the medium through which it becomes awakened.

It is surprising that Deleuze never comments on this passage (in *Kant's Critical Philosophy*, there is a quick mention of a "vital force," but no development of it[51]). It is surprising because we have here an intersection of concepts which Deleuze returned to again and again in his major works of the 60s: the body, life, and joy as the promotion of activity. And what is more, for Kant, all of these concepts are linked in an essential way even if the details of this intersection remain unclear. Were one to take Kant from behind and give him a monstrous offspring, this would be the place. But Deleuze does not do this. There is an immediate reason for this which Deleuze gave in his letter to Michel Cressole. While his texts in the history of philosophy generally include some buggery, Deleuze says his book on Kant "was different." *Kant's Critical Philosophy* is "a book about an enemy that tries to show how his system works, its various cogs."[52] This is perhaps one reason why Deleuze leaves this passage alone. It is possible to venture a more interesting thesis however. If we follow the workings of the various cogs in the third *Critique*, it becomes clear that Kant's initial association of aesthetic judgment with the body is almost immediately surpassed. Deleuze's reading of the third *Critique* emphasizes this immediate transcendence of the body in Kant whereas Deleuze's own aesthetics will rigorously assert the continuity of life, body and mind.

For Kant, the pleasure we experience in aesthetic judgment is not "gratification," as the passage quoted above might suggest. Gratification is merely "**animal**, i.e. bodily sensation."[53] But the aesthetic judgment is disinterested. It is rigorously uninterested in the object which is contemplated. As Rudolph Makkreel shows, this disinterest goes all the way down to the sensory organs. "Ordinary sensual and perceptual interests are suspended in aesthetic contemplation."[54] The pleasure we experience in the beautiful is that of the animation of our faculties. In the free play of imagination and understanding we feel our powers increase and we linger over this experience. The "Analytic of the Beautiful" then, points toward a sphere entirely independent of the body in which aesthetic pleasure unfolds. But what is this sphere or this element which is divided up by all of the faculties?

Deleuze will argue at the end of his reading of the third *Critique* that this sphere is nothing other than the faculty of judgment.[55] But his reading of the *Critique of Judgment* emphasizes the progressive development of this concept across Kant's text. Schematically, we might say that Deleuze shows Kant deepening his concept of the mind in three distinct stages which move it from an embodied mind to the very seat of our soul. The first iteration of the concept occurs at the end of the "The Analytic of the Beautiful" where Kant proposes for the first, but not the last time the idea of an aesthetic "common sense" to name this element.[56] The notion of common sense would have several virtues, Kant argues. Unlike the notion of the mind, the notion of a common sense would not have any "psychological" connotations.[57] It would also emphasize that this faculty in question would be common in double sense that it unites all of the other faculties,[58] and, more importantly, in the sense that it is something we all share by virtue of being human.[59] It would, thus, emphasize the universality of aesthetic judgments. Finally, the notion of sense would remind us that what is universal is precisely that feeling of pleasure we experience in the animation of our faculties. At this point in the *Critique*, however, Kant seems reluctant to actually posit such a principle. Common sense is "merely an ideal norm"[60] he says. And although he asserts the necessity of presupposing this norm in each of the last three sections of the first book, he concludes by claiming that "whether or not there is such a common sense, as a constitutive principle of the possibility of experience, or whether yet a higher principle of reason only makes it into a regulative principle . . .—this is something we would not and cannot yet investigate here."[61]

The next book, "The Analytic of the Sublime" takes up and deepens this notion. In the first form of the sublime, the "mathematical sublime," the imagination apprehends magnitudes and series which outstrip its capacity to comprehend them. Fatigued and exhausted, it gives up, and the mind temporarily experiences an inhibition of its powers, or an initial moment of "pain." But at this point, "the mind [*Gemüt*] hears in itself the voice of reason."[62] Reason steps in and provides us with the Idea of a whole which easily comprehends the magnitude. We thus realize with great pleasure that sublimity lies not in the object initially contemplated, but "in the mind of the one who judges."[63]

This raises two issues with respect to the development and deepening of the concepts of life and mind. First, reason enters the picture here as "a faculty of the mind which surpasses every standard of sense." It is a "faculty in the human mind that is itself supersensible."[64] It, thus, points toward a destination of thought which breaks radically from the sensible or the merely psychological. Second, it raises again, but with considerably more weight, the problem of an aesthetic common sense. In the same way the beautiful revealed an accord between the imagination and understanding, the sublime reveals an accord between reason and imagination. The problem raised by the judgment of taste—that there seemed to be an element in which imagination and understanding related freely to one another—is raised yet again, and this element now contains a faculty which transcends the sensible. All of these themes raised by the mathematical sublime are further intensified in Kant's account of the dynamic sublime.

In the dynamic sublime, we confront the power of nature over us. When we encounter bold, overhanging cliffs, monstrous thunder clouds, volcanoes, hurricanes, and other natural phenomena which threaten to immediately overcome our power to resist them, we are first afraid, but soon become aware of something within us which transcends their power.

> The sight of them only becomes all the more attractive the more fearful it is, as long as we find ourselves in safety, and we gladly call these objects sublime because they elevate the strength of our soul above its usual level, and allow us to discover within ourselves a capacity for resistance of quite another kind, which gives us the courage to measure ourselves against the apparent all-powerfulness of nature.[65]

Kant initially defined an aesthetic judgment as one in which the *mind* became conscious of its "state," the pleasure or pain felt in the activity or inhibition of its faculties. But in this passage, we become aware of our *soul*. It is the "strength" of our soul which is "elevated above its usual level" in the dynamic sublime, not that of our mind. Kant had kept these two concepts separate. In the "Transcendental Aesthetic" of the *Critique of Pure Reason*, for example, he sharply distinguished the mind from the soul, claiming that the mind can become conscious of itself, but not the soul.[66] Here, however, we do in fact feel our soul increase its strength. And Kant will even suggest that were we to succumb to nature we would still be aware of this higher destiny (the "humanity in our person remains undemeaned even though the human being must submit to that dominion"[67]). The dynamic sublime "calls forth our power (which is not part of nature)"[68] This represents a further deepening of the faculty of judgment, and pushes the problem of the mind into an entirely new territory for Deleuze.

The idea of genesis

Commenting on this passage, Deleuze writes, "the soul (*l'âme*) is felt as the indeterminate suprasensible unity of all the faculties; we ourselves are brought back to a focus, as a 'focal point' in the suprasensible."[69] This passage accomplishes, very quickly, two important things. It first reaffirms that what is *felt* is not the mind, but the soul. But, second, it identifies this soul as the point of unity for all of the faculties—in other words, it attributes to this formerly noumenal and thus inaccessible concept the major attribute of the mind. It is the element in which the mind and its faculties are united. Kant, himself, however does not make either of these claims at this particular point in the text. Deleuze is anticipating an argument he made most forcefully in his essay, "The Idea of Genesis in Kant's Esthetics."

Kant never explicitly returns to the question he raised at the end of the "Analytic of the Beautiful": do we posit aesthetic common sense as a merely regulative principle—that is, one which functions as a heuristic, allowing us to better organize experience—or do we posit it as a genuinely genetic or constitutive principle?[70] He certainly returns to the question of an aesthetic common sense, and, with the "Analytic of the Sublime" and its discoveries behind him, he asserts that there is indeed an aesthetic common sense and that it is nothing other than the faculty of judging itself which we rightly presuppose of everybody. But Kant does not raise the question as to whether this faculty is posited regulatively or genetically. Deleuze, however, does. He claims that the *Critique of Judgment* converges on the discovery of

> what Kant calls the Soul, that is, the supra-sensible unity of our faculties, 'the point of concentration', the life-giving principle that 'animates' each faculty, engendering both its free exercise and its free agreement with the other faculties. A primeval free imagination that cannot be satisfied with schematizing under the constraints of the understanding; a primeval unlimited understanding that does not yet bend under the speculative weight of its determinate concepts, no more so than it is not yet already subjected to the ends of practical reason; a primeval reason that has not yet developed a taste for commanding, but which frees itself when it frees up the other faculties—these are the extreme discoveries of the *Critique of Judgment*: each faculty rediscovers the principle of its genesis as each converges on this focal point, 'a point of concentration in the supra-sensible', whence our faculties take their force and their life.[71]

For Deleuze, this represents a "*ground* that had remained hidden in the other two Critiques,"[72] and the unveiling of this ground makes the *Critique of Judgment* itself, the "original ground from which derive the other two Critiques."[73]

His reading is grounded on two passages. Most of Deleuze's quotations here are from §49 in which Kant switches from the point of view to of the spectator to that of the artist, and discusses genius. Works of genius have "spirit," Kant says. Spirit is "the animating principle in the mind," it is what "animates the soul" and "sets the mental powers into motion." The genius is uniquely capable of creating works which accomplish this. Deleuze merges these claims with a crucial passage in §57. In his resolution of the antinomy of taste (which turns around the question of how is it we can argue about artworks when aesthetic judgments are nonconceptual), Kant argues that we have to give this unity of the faculties a metaphysical extension. One "is compelled, against one's will, to look beyond the sensible and to seek the unifying point of all our faculties *a priori* in the supersensible."[74]

determines."[78] (And, as I argued above, to limit this to *Nietzsche and Philosophy* would be a mistake. This principle is not just what Deleuze called there the "will to power." It is what he called in *Difference and Repetition*, the "spontaneous imagination," in *The Logic of Sense* and *Anti-Oedipus* the "body without organs," and in *Cinema I* and *II*, the interval or the body-hyphen in which images are selected, organized, and integrated back into the flux.) To what extent is this principle already in Kant's *Critique of Judgment*? And how does Deleuze's own genetic principle differ from the "soul," that supersensible and living unity which is the genetic element of our faculties?

The first way in which these two principles differ is with respect to heights and depths. Deleuze calls this focal point the "deepest point of the soul."[79] And insofar as it contains, at the level of the supersensible, our destiny as moral beings, it also points toward what is highest in us.[80] This focal point of all the faculties does "not merely constitute that which is *deepest* in the soul, but prepare[s] the advent of that which is *most elevated*."[81] But this is precisely the problem: this principle is located at the level of the supersensible. It is outside what Deleuze will call the outside.[82] We might say that this is a final sense in which Kant "endangered" the principle of synthesis. It's not simply that he moved it to a pure activity in the second edition of the first critique, and thereby removed the possibility of understanding it genetically.[83] In the third critique, and at the moment he is about to reveal a genuinely genetic principle, Kant locates that principle in another world, or, better, in a world which we can only hope is yet to come and whose realization will be the end of history.[84] Far from merging with life, then, it merges with what is other than life—an abstract moral destiny and an abstract larval subject. While the soul represents the genetic principle Deleuze had been looking for, it puts that principle outside of nature. As Foucault puts it in only a slightly different context, the further we follow the destiny of Kant's *Gemüt*, the more become enveloped in an "imperious cloak of spiritual sovereignty."[85]

If we compare this notion of the soul to Deleuze's own work, we can immediately see the first major difference then: for Deleuze, this substrate is not supersensible. It is not a noumenal focal point which stands above and beyond the phenomenal realm. Rather, the two are collapsed into one another. The principle of synthesis is strictly immanent to the sensible. For Deleuze, aesthetic judgment takes root in what Kant called "the animal" (and as Deleuze says in multiple late texts, aesthetic experience is inseparable from a becoming-animal). The will to power is power *of* life; the interval is dissolved in the plane of immanence; the body without organs is dissolved in the universal cesspool like a drop of wine in the ocean. As Deleuze puts it in *Difference and Repetition*, "art" does not catapult us outside of experience, but returns us to "the conditions of real experience.... It is here that we find the lived reality (*réalité vécue*) of a sub-representative domain."[86]

The second way in which Deleuze differs from Kant is in this insistence on genesis. Despite his claim that there were no hidden emissions in his reading of Kant, there does seem to be a minor slippage here.[87] Deleuze claims that in aesthetic judgment, we discover a "primeval (*originelle*)" imagination, a "primeval" understanding and a "primeval" reason, gathered together in a genetic element which will be awakened through a "transcendental Culture."[88] As Rudolph Gasché, among others, persuasively argues, we do not exactly discover *primeval* faculties. Rather we discover an element in which the faculties are isolated at their highest point of *activity*.[89] In aesthetic judgments, according to Kant, we are concerned with fully developed faculties in the prime of their functioning. In aesthetic judgments, according to Deleuze, we are concerned with faculties in a larval state. These two readings are not necessarily opposed, but this movement toward undeveloped or underdeveloped faculties would require a more robust defense of the narrative from *Gemüt* to soul than the one I developed here. These arguments, however, are much more interesting to the extent that they orient us with respect to Deleuze's own thought.

Aesthetics

If we pursue this latter route, we ultimately have to ask where all of this leaves aesthetics? This question is obviously too big to answer exhaustively here. But whatever we say about this will revolve around a provocative claim Deleuze makes in *Difference and Repetition*. By searching for the conditions of possible experience rather than those of real experience, Deleuze claims, Kant divided aesthetics into two parts. The conditions of possible experience

> are too general or too large for the real. The net is so loose that the largest fish pass through No wonder, then, that aesthetics should be divided into two irreducible domains: that of the theory of the sensible which captures only the real's conformity with possible experience; and that of the theory of the beautiful which deals with the reality of the real in so far as it is thought.[90]

The real is missed in two ways here. In *The Critique of Pure Reason*, it is missed because it shunted into the forms of space and time which make it susceptible to imaginative synthesis regulated by the categories. In *The Critique of Judgment*, it is missed insofar as the abyss which it reveals only reveals in turn a disembodied soul. Deleuze cites the Analytic of the Beautiful here, and the disinterest of aesthetic judgment, but Kant is even more explicit about this, we saw, in the Analytic of the Sublime where he says that it is not nature that is sublime but "only in the mind of the one who judges."[91]

If, however, we try to think a genuinely genetic principle which is no wider than its conditioned, then, this has decisive consequences for aesthetics.

> Everything changes once we determine the conditions of real experience, which are not larger than the conditioned and which differ in kind from the categories: the two senses of the aesthetic become one, to the point where the being of the sensible reveals itself in the work of art, while at the same time the work of art appears as experimentation.[92]

Aesthetics, as a theory of the beautiful, collapses into aesthetic as the theory of the sensible, and this has consequences for both art and perception. The immediate consequence, and the one Deleuze seems to highlight here, is the one I have already mentioned twice in this chapter: art tells us about subjectivity at the same time that subjectivity explains art. But the consequences seem to go well beyond this explanatory matrix.

As evidenced by Deleuze's ethics, pleasure and pain are still very operative concepts. But they no longer refer to a specifically aesthetic experience. They are ways we evaluate all of experience. The good is what increases my power of life, and the bad is what hinders it, and this seems to diminish the specificity or the aesthetic and open it up to the plurality of everyday experience. Kant was already gesturing in this direction himself in his constant use of examples from nature to characterize beauty and sublimity and in his annexation of the theory of teleological judgment to aesthetic judgment. But Deleuze goes further. When the two halves of the aesthetic are united, we are no longer capable of disinterested contemplation. As he says in *Nietzsche and Philosophy*, "Art is the opposite of a 'disinterested' operation: it does not heal, calm, sublimate or pay off, it does not 'suspend' desire, instinct or will. On the contrary, art is a 'stimulant of the will to power', 'something that excites willing.'"[93] This is still Kantian. It is still a question of the stimulation of our power of life. But this stimulation is no longer disinterested. It bears directly on our perceptual processes. This is what I have argued here in my reading of *Cinema I* and *II*. The theory of subjectivity which structures the book is indeed that of the artist, the spectator, and the fictional Marcel. It is also that of the ordinary individual.

But this raises the question as to whether there is anything specific to art. It would seem that there is in that, unlike Kant, Deleuze's aesthetics consistently deal with actual art—from Proust to Sacher-Masoch to Kafka to Francis Bacon to the whole of cinema up until 1983. *Cinema I* and *II*, in particular, suggest a possible answer to this question in the close relationship they establish between cinema and the body.[94] Our body produces links between images as it goes about its daily business. But cinema also produces links between images, and this invention of new relations is the particular vocation of the artist or the artistic will. As Deleuze says in *Cinema II*, cinema finds its "essence" or "vocation" in its capacity to invent new ways of connecting images. "The greatness of modern cinema," writes Paola Marrati, "lies in its capability to create other links"[95] and "new ways of connecting images."[96] Although these new links or formal connections are created by the artist, they do not merely exist on film or on the canvas. Because the two halves of the aesthetic are united in Deleuze's thought, and because the work of art does, for Deleuze, bear directly on the "nervous system" or the "will to power," we

AESTHETICS

have to say that these new ways of linking images *supervene on our perceptual processes*. Deleuze is very clear about this: cinema's images have the capacity to be "*introduced into sensory-motor linkages*" and they themselves "*organize or induce these linkages*."[97] Every image, from this point of view, while organized by the artist, is also an "organization" of our sensory-motor schema. The kinds of judgments we make about artworks, then, relate to the ways of seeing, feeling, and acting which images create. Hence, Deleuze's claim that cinema creates new "possibilities of life" and "new ways of living." As Paola Marrati puts it, cinema's images are "other livable configurations of thought."[98] In this way, aesthetics becomes what Guattari called "ethico-aesthetics."

Composition, sensation, territory

We might, from this point of view, return to the three quotations I started with. All three quotations are still functional and provocative from this point of view, but they take on a depth and an extension which was missing when they stood alone as disconnected passages functioning more or less as *ex cathedra* statements on the nature of art.

The first, "Composition, composition is the sole definition of art,"[99] emphasizes the formal nature of Deleuze's aesthetics, or the emphasis on the linkages between and within images. But this attention to form is not merely aesthetic. It is also a major characteristic of his account of perception. We can see this if we note that "composition" is a complex word in this context. What Deleuze and Guattari directly mean in *What is Philosophy?* is simply that art pertains to what they call the "plane of composition." But Deleuze and Guattari's use of the word "composition" here is an allusion to Deleuze's earlier reading of Spinoza. In *Expressionism in Philosophy*, Deleuze had repeatedly characterized the material field of extensive parts as a field of composition. Extensive parts enter into their characteristic relations on this plane according to the laws of movement and rest. "Composition," then, refers simultaneously to the way in which I organize my affections (or am organized by them) and to the way in which a work of art is composed. To say that composition is the sole definition of art, then, is precisely to say that art is defined by its form, but, further, that this form is simultaneously formed and formative.

This position is captured in the second quotation. "The work of art" is "*a bloc of sensations, that is to say a compound of percepts and affects.*"[100] The characteristic relation which emerges from the plane of composition is the relation which structures a mode's extensive parts, and which changes according to the modification which this mode undergoes (it is a plastic form). It is thus a certain relation which gathers together the mode's modifications, its affections or perceptions. But, as a bloc of sensations, or as a particular organization of sensation, art shapes the way we see the world. A work contains within its composition ways of seeing, feeling, acting and thinking which, while products of an artistic will, supervene on the perceptual processes of its spectators. For this reason, the third quotation, in a way, encapsulates this entire process insofar as it points to the capacity of art to reorganize the world. "Can this becoming, this emergence [of a territory] be called Art? That would make the territory a result of art. The artist: the first person to set out a boundary stone, or to make a mark."[101]

5

Politics

Everything is political, but every politics is simultaneously a macropolitics *and a* micropolitics.[1]

Good or Bad, politics and its judgments are always molar, but it is the molecular and its assessment that makes or breaks it.[2]

Every institution imposes a series of models on our bodies, even in its involuntary structures, and offers our intelligence a sort of knowledge, a possibility of foresight as project.[3]

In the previous two chapters, I argued that Deleuze's ethics and his aesthetics play off of one another. The task of ethics is the production of an active and free subject, and thus the main work of ethics is the pursuit of new possibilities for life which make this possible. But this invention of new ways of existing was also the end of Deleuze's aesthetics. The artist is not someone who speaks only to himself or to a small coterie of sympathetic minds scattered across time; nor is the spectator disinterested, ambling from work to work with appreciative smiles and occasional "hmmmm's." The artist and the spectator are immediately *interested*. The work bears, as Deleuze says in *Francis Bacon*, directly on our nervous system.

It gives structure, as he argues in *Cinema I* and *Cinema II*, to the interval between perception and reaction and thereby shapes both our perceptions and our actions. In this way, it provides us with ways of being, of interpreting our world and of acting.

My basic claim in this chapter is that Deleuze's politics brings these two points of view together. There is an aesthetics of politics, and there is an ethics of politics. There is an aesthetics of politics in that political institutions bear directly on the most fundamental levels of subjectivity and as a consequence they structure the way we see the world.[4] There is an ethics of politics insofar as those political institutions are good which promote ways of life which increase the activity and freedom of the subjects gathered under them. Put differently, my basic contention here is that Deleuze's political philosophy has to be understood—as was the case for both his aesthetics and ethics—in relation to the articulation of subjectivity grounding his ontology (which I described in Chapter 2 above). The political is played out at each of the subject's three levels: molecular primary organization or passivity; secondary organization or creative thought; and the molar tertiary organization or propositional/representational thought.[5]

To make this point, the heart of this chapter is dedicated to a reactivation of the notion of the institution in Deleuze's early writings. This reading of Deleuze risks being immediately undermined by a common narrative we usually construct about the arc of Deleuze's work. It is most succinctly put by Michael Hardt in one of the earliest but still one of the best readings of Deleuze. Hardt explains that in two book-length texts from 1953—*Empiricism and Subjectivity* and *Instincts et institutions* (hereafter *Instincts and Institutions*)—we can see "the general outlines of a philosophical and political project beginning to take shape as a theory of the institution." "However," Hardt continues, "the general development of Deleuze's thought does not immediately follow this line; it becomes clear that Deleuze requires an extensive ontological detour before arriving at [his] positive political project."[6] The more popular but less precise version of this story is simply that Deleuze was concerned primarily with ontological questions until he met Guattari, at which point he began to be concerned with political questions. For reasons I sketched in the first chapter of this book, I do not subscribe to either version of this narrative, and as I will try to make clear below, not only is it the case that the theory of the institution provides the model for *Anti-Oedipus* and *A Thousand Plateaus*, but it also provides us with a more nuanced view of the process of strategic social assemblage.

Rousseau

One way of addressing this narrative problem (and simultaneously prefiguring some of the issues at stake here) is to install ourselves right in the middle of the gap between *Empiricism and Subjectivity* (1953) and *Nietzsche and Philosophy* (1962). Despite Deleuze's claims in interviews that this period was a kind of hole in his career, this was far from an inactive period. One of the central documents remaining from it is a set of notes for a 1960 course he gave at the Sorbonne on Rousseau. Unlike most of the lectures we have access too—which are transcriptions of what Deleuze actually said—Deleuze's course notes on Rousseau are schematic and occasionally elliptical outlines of what he probably said, so it would obviously be imprudent to draw any definitive conclusions from them. One thing we can do, however, is note the presence of two lines of flight in this document: one looking ahead to his later work, the other looking back to *Empiricism and Subjectivity* and *Instincts and Institutions*.

Deleuze's lecture begins and ends with a more or less standard discussion of the concept of the social contract. He distinguishes it from the Hobbesian version, he explains the concept of the general will, he works through the problem of the legislator, and so on. The social contract, Deleuze says, is "the act" by which we "constitute ourselves as political subjects." The entire question of middle sections of the lecture is how such an act is possible. His course, then, is an enquiry into the conditions of political subjectivity.[7]

At the end of the lecture, he neatly summarizes the entire process. It is only from the point of view of genesis, Deleuze argues, we can finally grasp both the constitution of political subjectivity and the unity of Rousseau's work. Here is his schema:

- physical species and physical individuality = beautiful harmony
- genetic point of view

from physical passivity to physical activity
　　　from physical activity to moral species
　– Man as a moral species,[8] but a rupture of the individual with the species
　　　Discourse on Inequality: deception of the one by the others
　　　Nouvelle Héloïse: self-deception
　– Moral act of will which reestablishes a subjective unity between the individual and the species: the *Confessions* and the second part of the *Nouvelle Héloïse*.
　– Determination of a political act which establishes the objective unity of the individual and the moral species: the "*Social Contract*."[9]

It is hard to imagine what Deleuze would have said around these points, because there are so many confusing (but fascinating) aspects of this list as it stands—starting with the absence of *Emile* and ending with the deployment of the Kantian concept of a "moral species." The basic itinerary, however, is clear. In the state of nature, the individual is in harmony with the species. As we develop our physical and moral capacities, we fall from this state of harmony through a genesis which carries us from our physical being to a state of moral being, and from moral being to a decisive political act: the contract. The last three stages are interesting from the point of view of Rousseau's *oeuvre*. The first two, insofar as they indicate a process of becoming active and thus seem to anticipate the ethics of *Nietzsche and Philosophy* and *Expressionism in Philosophy*, are interesting from the point of view of Deleuze's.

Earlier in the lecture, Deleuze focuses on these initial stages of the genesis. He structures the conversation around the notion of perfectibility in the second *Discourse*. Rousseau's basic idea is that natural man is in possession of all of his faculties and social virtues, but, in the state of nature, these faculties remain in a state of potentiality. They require the intervention of circumstance to pull them out of their latency, develop them, and thereby send us on our way to social being. Here is how Rousseau puts it the second *Discourse*: "the social virtues and the other faculties which natural man had received in potentiality (*en puissance*) could never develop by themselves . . . in order to do so, they needed the fortuitous concatenations of several foreign causes . . . ."[10] In the state of nature, all of our faculties are there, in potential, like lines in a block of marble; as a consequence of fortuitous encounters certain of the faculties become awakened and we become gradually perfected.

Deleuze provides the following gloss on this passage: "Notion of perfectibility: the state of nature must be understood as a genetic element, laden with potentialities, virtualities."[11] The basic idea remains the same, but Deleuze translates Rousseau into the philosophical vocabulary he would soon put to work in *Nietzsche and Philosophy*. This is not to say that there is anything illegitimate about moving from Rousseau's "*en puissance*" to Deleuze's "*potentialité*" and "*virtualitié*." All three terms were common translations of the Aristotelian notion of potential (though the last is considerably less common). But there is nothing innocent about it either, and Deleuze continues throughout the lecture to refer to the state of nature as a "virtual and genetic state"[12] from which man and ultimately society are developed.

Deleuze does not develop this genesis in anything like the detail we've seen in *Expressionism in Philosophy*, *Cinema 1* and *2* or the major texts of his middle period. But he does make some interesting notes which we can speculate on here. The first simply develops, through a rough outline, the original position of this genesis. The passage from virtuality to actuality, he says,

> . . . is not a spontaneous passage.
> In the discourse:
> – a faculty is not developed if it does not respond to a need or an interest;
> – a need is never perceived if it is not determined by a situation.
> The state of man must thus be defined:
> – by its objective circumstances
> – by the needs which determine it
> – by the subjective faculties necessary for the satisfaction of those needs.[13]

There are three basic terms, then, at the foundation of this genesis: man as a set of virtualities, the objective situation which elicits responses from man by provoking his needs, and the faculty which is produced in the interaction of these first two as a means of satisfying needs. The concept of faculty refers back to its literal meaning, a power or a capacity, a means to an end, and a network of needs determines those ends.

We cannot draw any rigorous conclusions from this. But we can say, at a minimum, that Deleuze's lecture on Rousseau seems to experiment with two basic questions. The first inquires into the conditions of political subjectivity. At a minimum, it presupposes a process of perfectibility, or what I called in Chapter 3, "a perfectionist ethics;" it presupposes—in *Deleuze's Rousseau*—a process of becoming active at the end of which we will become capable of the "decisive act." But, second, since Deleuze's description of this process already betrays a fundamental torsion in philosophical vocabulary, we have to wonder whether or not he has already called into question the *nature* of this decisive act and its conditions. Is the act by which we constitute ourselves as subjects a contract? And whether or not it is, can we think the conditions of that act in relation to an different conception of virtuality?

I will return to both of these questions below. The reason I turned to this lecture, though, is that it calls into question basic narratives we tell about Deleuze's intellectual itinerary. This lecture pushes us in two temporal directions: forward to Deleuze's works of the 60s, and backward to his works of the 50s. In relation to the major texts of the 60s, we might note that this concern with faculties, and their successive awakening, was something which would preoccupy Deleuze over the course of the next decade. It was a central problem in *Proust & Signs* (1964), it resurfaced in *Difference and Repetition* (1968) as one of the many formulations of passive synthesis, and it was at the heart of his innovative reading of Spinoza (as I argued in Chapter 3) in *Expressionism in Philosophy*. Along these lines, we might also note that the appearance in Deleuze's Rousseau lecture of a "virtual and genetic state" means that his concern with virtuality and genetic principles was not something which appeared in 1962 with *Nietzsche and Philosophy* and lasted throughout the 60s.[14] (And this occurrence in Rousseau is not even the first: we find the concepts already operative in Deleuze's important 1956 essays on Bergson and in his 1956 lecture series *What is Grounding?*)

In the other direction, looking back from the Rousseau lecture to Deleuze's two major texts already in existence—*Empiricism and Subjectivity* (1953) and *Instincts and Institutions* (1953)—we cannot help but notice the central role of the concept of *need* in the lecture. It is need which "determines" the state of man, and it is the attempt to satisfy those needs which awaken each faculty. In addition to referring us forward to the Deleuze of the 60s, then, this text also refers us back to the Deleuze of the 50s, and in particular, to two major texts that appeared in 1953. In both of these texts, Deleuze elaborated a theory of the institution as the indirect and social satisfaction of needs.

Hume

The theory of the institution in *Empiricism and Subjectivity* has often been overlooked as a serious contribution to Deleuze's political philosophy. This is for several reasons, not the least of which is that *Empiricism and Subjectivity* itself has been more or less rigorously ignored by Deleuze studies.[15] But on top of this, we also seem not to have acknowledged just how far Deleuze pushed Hume with respect to the theory of the institution. Deleuze's regular endorsements of Hume's positions (Hume's vision of "society is very strong;" it is grounded in the "principle of all serious political philosophy;" Hume has discovered the very "meaning of government"), when set alongside Deleuze's equally regular extension of the Humean notion of the institution, suggests that this strong vision of society is not exactly Hume's.

As in his lecture notes on Rousseau, and as in *Expressionism in Philosophy*, Deleuze begins by putting strong limitations on the notion of the social contract. He regularly claims that it promotes a negative, limiting, and abstract notion of society. These criticisms are grounded in Hume's own well-known criticisms of the concept. Hume levied a whole series of complaints against the contract. It is first of all logically contradictory insofar as the act which supposedly founds society in fact presupposes the existence and functioning of society., It is also historically and empirically insufficient: there never actually was a contract (not even following revolutions); governments are historically established through usurpation or conquest, not consent.[16] Further, the concept of tacit consent is itself a bad concept because it presupposes the person has a choice, but "can we seriously say, that a poor peasant or artisan has a free choice to leave his country, when he knows no foreign language or manners, and lives, from day to day, by the small wages which he acquires?."[17] What we should acknowledge, Hume argued, is that our entrance into society is an involuntary act and that society itself finds its origin in violence and force: The original establishment was formed by violence, and submitted to from necessity. The subsequent administration is also supported by power, and acquiesced in by the people, not as a matter of choice, but of obligation."[18] Deleuze affirmed all of these criticisms of the contract in *Empiricism and Subjectivity*, but his development of the theory of the institution is grounded on another text.

In his much earlier *Treatise of Human Nature*, and in the context of a conjectural rather than empirical history, Hume emphasized another motivation for our entrance into society: utility. Section two of book three, "Of the Origin of Justice and Property," begins with this observation: "Of all the animals, with which this globe is peopl'd, there is none toward whom nature seems, at first sight, to have excercis'd more cruelty than towards man . . . ." Nature has overburdened us with needs and wants but at the same time has failed to supply us with the means of relieving these necessities. To achieve satisfaction of even our most basic needs, we need to invent an artificial means. This is the most general function of society for Hume. "'Tis by society alone [man] is able to supply his defects . . . . By society all his infirmities are compensated." Hume thus immediately establishes the basic function of society as means of satisfying basic needs. Where nature shortchanged us at the level of instinct, artifice steps in and satisfies our basic necessities.[19]

For Hume, the theory of the institution is a response to two basic problems which arise within the circuit of need and satisfaction: partiality—or limited generosity—and scarcity, or the fact that there are not enough social goods to supply everyone's desires and necessities. Deleuze emphasizes the first of these. The basic political problem is not *self*-interest, but limited interest: nature has constructed things such that I care only about those closest to me.

The basic problem of society, then, is not how to limit my self-interest but how to *extend* and *integrate* my limited sympathy. "The problem of society ... is not a problem of limitation, but rather a problem of integration. To integrate sympathies is to make sympathy transcend its ... natural partiality (ES 40). The institution is the mechanism which accomplishes this positive integration.

In *Empiricism and Subjectivity*, Deleuze develops three central characteristics of institutions: they are fictional; they work by positing ends; these ends "reflect" passions and thereby "integrate" them. First, every institution is grounded in an act of the imagination. The basic condition of integration is an act of the imagination. "[I]ntegration implies a positive moral world, and is brought about by the positive invention of such a world" (ES 40). (We thus find here one of the basic propositions of Deleuze's ethics and aesthetics: the necessity to imagine new possibilities for life.) Second, Deleuze seems to suggest that we institute by determining ends. What is invented is not the product of any ordinary noncausal synthesis. What Deleuze usually says is that we produce a "whole": "the moral world requires the constitution of a whole, of society" (40). Or, "one can only invent a whole" (40).[20] But Deleuze provocatively and all-too-quickly maps the part-whole relationship onto the means-end relationship,[21] so another way of saying this is to say that we invent this or that *end* capable of integrating partial ends:

> The moral world is the artificial totality wherein particular ends are integrated and added to one another. Or again, the moral world is the system of means which allow my particular interest, and also the interest of the other, to be satisfied and realized. (ES 41)

This is the most Deleuze says about the internal structure of an institution in this text: it is centered around an end capable of integrating the interests of its constituent members. This artificial and invented end, once constructed, takes on the form of a "model of action" or a "rule or a norm" (ES 41), and the function of this rule is organize the institution. "Justice is not a principle of nature; it is rather a *rule*, a law of construction and its role is to organize, within a whole, the elements [of morality], including principles of nature" (ES 40; original emphasis).

Finally, this organization works by means of what Deleuze calls "reflection." To call this artifice a rule implies that there is something abstract and prescriptive about it, as though the way it worked was by posing a transcendent principle which we must follow whether or not we like it. Nothing could be further from the case. Deleuze quotes a passage from the *Treatise of Human Nature* in which Hume argues that one cannot control self-interest, or "the interested affection;" rather, all we can do it divert its course: "There is no passion . . . capable of controlling the interested affection, but the very affection itself, by an alteration of its direction. Now this alteration must necessarily take place upon the least reflection." This is a difficult passage to interpret in both Hume's English and in the translation Deleuze was reading. Deleuze provides this gloss on the passage: "We must understand that justice is not a reflection *on* interest, but rather a reflection *of* interest, a kind of twisting of the passion itself in the mind affected by it." Deleuze does not develop this with the kind of detail we might like here. The basic point, though, seems to be that the institution functions at the level of the passions, and in so doing, works by structuring our very capacity to feel—or to use the language of the later Deleuze, this process of organization by means of reflection is a kind of segmentation and territorialization. It is a kind of social schematism.

This intrusion of the institution into the realm of the passions or the micropolitical is perhaps *the* central feature of institutions in *Empiricism and Subjectivity*. It explains how an institution can be understood as a satisfaction of need, but also how, in satisfying needs and by redirecting the passions, institutions *alter* our needs and perceptions. In redirecting our interests, Deleuze explains later, the institution "adds many other motives to interest—motives that are often contradictory (prodigality, ignorance, heredity, custom, habit, or 'sprit of greed and endeavor, of luxury and abundance')" (ES 45). The conclusion he draws from this, in sweeping italics, is that "*Dispositions (la tendance) are never abstracted from the means which we organize in order to satisfy them*" (ES 45). This means, first of all that there is an immanence of institution and "tendency," but second of all, and as a consequence of this, that what we organize in order to satisfy our tendency—the institution—does not simply satisfy that drive; it shapes it and gives it its basic characteristics.

This sounds ominous, and it induces (for me at least) a reflexive repulsion and a desire to find a noninstitutional mode of existence. But for Deleuze's Hume, this is, strictly speaking, impossible. We enter into institutions because we cannot satisfy our needs without them. Institutions are invented means for the satisfaction of a tendency. The central political task, Deleuze will suggest in *Instincts and Institutions*, his other major text of this period, is to ensure that they provide us with new possibilities for life which secure our freedom.

I began this section with the claim that Deleuze pushes Hume in the direction of concepts Hume was not using and questions he was not asking. There are at least two ways he does this. The first is that Deleuze is clearly extending the notion of the institution to areas Hume did not. When we talk about institutions in Hume, we usually mean things like property, family, promises, and broad governmental institutions. Deleuze references these, but he also says that he is interested in social institutions—not governmental (47)—including smaller "communities," forms of "friendship" and "neighborliness" (38). At one point, he asserts the congruence of these arguments with the discoveries of "ethnography" (48). The second and related instance is Deleuze's insistence on using statements like, "a drive (*tendance*) is satisfied inside an institution" (46) or "the satisfaction of human drives (*tendances*) is related, not to the drive (*tendance*) itself, but rather to the reflected drive (*tendance*). This is the meaning of the institution . . ." (49). As the second chapter of *Empiricism and Subjectivity* evolves (and as the name Bergson continues to appear), the institution becomes less and less a satisfaction of *needs* and a reflection of *passions* than a satisfaction and reflection of *tendencies*.

To make sense of these gestures we need to turn to Deleuze's second major text of 1953, *Instincts and Institutions*. In this text we find both a clarification of what Deleuze means by "*tendance*" and a fuller version of his understanding of institutions.

Instincts and Institutions

To call *Instincts and Institutions* a "major text" seems itself like an overextension of the work. Not only has this text received very little attention in the secondary literature on Deleuze, but at first sight, there does not seem to be much Deleuze in it at all: with the exception of a short introduction, this 84-page text is merely the assemblage of other texts. It is part of an interesting series directed by Georges Canguilhem. Canguilhem explains in his introduction to the series that his basic motivation was to provide students of all levels access to foundational texts surrounding basic philosophical problems. To achieve this end, he asked mostly young scholars (and mostly scholars who were completing a degree under him) to edit a number of volumes which would collect the essential historical and contemporary documents related to a given problem. Thus, there were books on language, freedom, the unconscious, science and logic, affection and feeling, and life and culture, among others. Canguilhem himself edited *Besoins et tendances*.

To say that *Instincts and Institutions* is a collection of important texts selected by Deleuze, however, suggests that Deleuze simply cut and pasted various passages related to the general theme of instincts and institutions. This is far from the case. Deleuze was a remarkably creative (and often intrusive) editor. The texts he selected were a mixture of well-known and unexpected writers from both well-established and obscure traditions. More importantly, the order he put these texts in was far from innocent. He shaped everything into a complex narrative which is indicated by his table of contents, his section headings, and in the titles he gave each extract. And finally, he consistently altered the passages he quoted, often tearing them from their context and altering their wording—sometimes for clarity but sometimes just to make a point more forcefully. Although this text is a collection of other texts, it is also itself a carefully constructed and crafted document. Finding Deleuze's voice in this is difficult, but not impossible.

Appearing in 1953, alongside *Empiricism and Subjectivity*, and three years before the publication of his two early essays on Bergson, *Instincts and Institutions* obviously develops the Humean emphasis on the political importance of institutions and the ways in which institutions reconfigure the basic structures of subjectivity. But the first thing one notices is that there are only two short excerpts from Hume. Malinowski, Levi-Strauss, and Maurice Hauriou, a French jurist who developed an important theory of law,[22] are all quoted more frequently. And it is arguable, for reasons discussed below, that the most imposing figure here is Bergson. This book is not a brief aftershock of *Empiricism and Subjectivity* then. It is a transposition of the arguments Deleuze outlined in Hume to an entirely different level. Or, put differently, *Instincts and Institutions* can be read as replaying of Humean political philosophy on a loosely (and thus not exclusively) Bergsonian stage—and this implies at least two things. It means first of all that the political philosophy Deleuze outlined in Hume is one which attracted him and which he continued to *develop*. Second, if the operative concepts which emerge across this text fit both Hume and Bergson, it's likely that they're not specific to either, or, in other words, that what we witness in this text is the gradual development of the foundations of Deleuze's own political philosophy.

Tendency

The central question of the book is no doubt Humean in nature—what is the relation between instincts and institutions?—and Deleuze returns to some of the basic points he made about institutions in *Empiricism and Subjectivity*. "What we call an instinct and what we call an institution essentially designate procedures of satisfaction" he writes in his introduction to the volume; these are the two "organized forms of a possible satisfaction" (DI 20). And, as in *Empiricism and Subjectivity*, what calls for satisfaction is both "needs" and "*tendencies*." This structured relationship between tendency, instinct, and institution is not articulated or developed by any of the passages Deleuze excerpts. It is something he has imposed on the text and consistently reinforced throughout. Chapter 1, for example, is called "The Institution: System of Indirect and Social Means for Satisfying a Tendency." Chapter 2 is entitled "Instinct: System of Direct and Specific for Satisfying a Tendency." It is clear that both instincts and institutions are means of satisfying a tendency. An instinct is a direct satisfaction of a tendency; an institution is an indirect satisfaction of a tendency. But what, then, is a tendency?

There is not one excerpt which directly discusses the meaning of this concept. There is, however, a footnote on page 13 which offers a hint. There Deleuze writes, "for the Freudian conception of instinct and tendency," we should consult excerpt 39 of Canguilhem's contribution to the series, *Besoins et tendances*. The passage to which Deleuze refers is an excerpt from Freud's *Introductory Lectures on Psychoanalysis*. As Christian Kerslake has helpfully pointed out, "*tendance*" was an early translation of the Freudian concept of "drive" (before *pulsion* became the dominant).[23] This seems to be one of the most basic senses in which Deleuze uses the notion of tendency here—in particular, the way he distinguishes it from instinct and need—and it is worth briefly developing. Lacan, responding to the English mistranslation of Freud's "*Trieb*" as "instinct," consistently differentiated instinct and drive (and, in a move which will become important below, gave it an ontological extension[24]). Instinct, for example, is species-specific and remains more or less constant across a life; drives, on the other hand, are capable of dramatic alterations in relation to each person's history, and particularly during the first few years of that history. More profoundly, for Lacan, the notion of a drive is fundamentally nonbiological, and has nothing to do with the "organism," with a "biological function," or with "the pressure of a need" such as hunger or thirst.[25] Needs are instinctually and therefore more or less immediately and directly satisfied by their objects. When you are thirsty, you drink; when you are hungry, you eat. A drive (or tendency), however, is satisfied indirectly, and thus, the object which satisfies the drive is of little importance. "*As far as the object of the drive is concerned, let us be clear that it is, strictly speaking, a matter of no importance. It is a matter of total indifference*," Lacan says.[26] What does this mean? "[F]or the moment, I am not fucking, I am talking to you. Well! I can have exactly the same satisfaction as if I were fucking. That's what it means. Indeed, it raises the question of whether in fact I am not fucking at this moment."[27] And thus, to characterize the drive, he uses the following expression: "The best formula seems to me to be the following—that *la pulsion en fait le tour*. . . . *Tour* is to be understood here with the ambiguity it possesses in French, both *turn*, the limit around which one turns, and *trick*."[28] The drive, then, is a tendency toward an object which it permanently turns around, but whose actual identity is unimportant and may as well be something else.

This Freudian subtext is no doubt present in *Instincts and Institutions*. The Deleuzian concept of tendency unquestionably has the sense of an ontological pulsion toward an undefined object. But the proximity of these two terms—instinct and tendency—alongside the overall structure of the text, suggests a further influence. Tendency is a concept which recurs throughout Bergson's work. It is most prominent in *Creative Evolution*. In this text, it seems to have two distinct, but related usages—one epistemological, the other ontological. Bergson seems, at times, to insist on a purely definitional conception of tendency. "A [geometrically] perfect definition applies only to a *completed* reality; now, vital properties are never entirely realized, though always on the way to become so; they are not so much *states* as *tendencies*."[29] Bergson draws on the notion of tendency here to characterize the kind of definition adequate to vital things, things in a state of permanent becoming. We cannot define them in terms of states without entirely missing the point. This is what Bergson calls a "static definition."[30] What the notion of tendency lets us think is a state of open development and permanent becoming. It thus provides us with the conceptual means of articulating a "dynamic definition."[31]

But as the text develops, the notion of tendency begins to take on much more important ontological function, and eventually comes to characterize the complex impulsion of the *élan vital* itself.[32] If life is an *explosive* force, it is because it contains within itself, an "unstable balance of tendencies."[33] This instability is the motor of a radically asymmetrical dialectic. As these contradictory forces play off of one another, life explodes into its various directions and species. "Life *is* tendency," Bergson writes, "and the essence of a tendency is to develop in the form of a sheaf, creating, by its very growth, divergent directions among which its impetus is divided."[34] Tendency, thus, explains the complication, in an original unity, of the various directions of life itself before they split off into various sub-tendencies—vegetative torpor, instinct and intelligence, and so on.

In the two essays on Bergson which immediately followed *Instincts and Institutions*, Deleuze pursued this latter, ontological, usage of the term and consistently characterized Bergson's thought as though there were two and only two tendencies: duration and matter. Of these two, the first was by far the most important to the extent that it encompassed the latter (DI 27). If we pursue this line of thought, Deleuze argues, we ultimately end up positing "time" as "substance."

Bergson's thesis could be summed up in this way: real time is alteration, and alteration is substance. Difference of nature is therefore no longer between two things or rather two tendencies; difference of nature is itself a thing, a tendency opposed to some other tendency. . . . Duration or tendency is the difference of self with itself . . . .

In Deleuze's hands, Bergson's conception of tendency ultimately means one thing: time, the principle of difference from which we must understand life. If we read tendency in this direction, the question of *Instincts and Institutions* becomes even more interesting. It is not simply a question of how institutions reflect instinct and indirectly satisfy desires. It is a question of how they structure time.

How far are we from the Freudian conception of drive? Potentially miles, but, as I will suggest below, one of the central accomplishments of Deleuze's thought in the 60s was to unite precisely these two points of view by grounding the production of time in a theory of the drive. This detour through the concept of tendency, then, will allow us to connect this discussion with Deleuze's later work.

Institution

The first chapter of *Instincts and Institutions* is titled, as I mentioned above, "The Institution: System of Indirect and Social Means for Satisfying a Tendency." In this chapter title, we get the basic definition of an institution as it was developed in *Empiricism and Subjectivity*: an institution is the social satisfaction of needs and tendencies. The chapter itself is broken into three parts: "Analysis of the Institution;" "Institution and Utility;" and "The Original Order of the Institution." Each part significantly develops the notion of the institution Deleuze had developed in Hume, and it what follows, I will describe them one at a time.

I argued above that in *Empiricism and Subjectivity* Deleuze had already extended the Humean theory of the institution well beyond the domain Hume had in mind, and in particular, to "ethnography." That passage in *Empiricism and Subjectivity* oddly suggests that the ethnographer Deleuze had in mind was Bergson. The opening passages of *Instincts and Institutions* engage with actual ethnographers. Deleuze begins with a long quotation from Malinowski's *Sex and Repression in Savage Society*—to which he appended the title "How the institution satisfies a tendency." I will quote the passage in full because *Instincts and Institutions* is not readily available.

1 How the institution satisfies a tendency.[35]

Thus the signal for courtship (*le besoin du rapprochement sexuel*), the release of the process of mating, is given not by a mere bodily change [as in apes] but [in man] by a combination of cultural influences. In the last instance these influences obviously act upon the human body and stimulate innate reactions in that they provide physical proximity [between young people], mental atmosphere, and appropriate suggestions; unless the organism were ready to respond sexually no cultural institutions could make man mate. But, instead of an automatic physiological mechanism, we have a complicated arrangement (*dispositif*) into which artificial elements have been largely introduced. Two points, therefore, must be noted: there is no purely biological release mechanism in man, but instead there is a combined psychological and physiological process determined in its temporal, spatial and formal nature by cultural tradition; associated with it and supplementing it is a system of cultural taboos which limit considerably the working of the sexual impulse.

... While in animals we find a chain of linked instincts succeeding each other and replacing each other, human behaviour is defined by a fully organized emotional attitude, a *sentiment*, ... In man, culture creates a new need, the need to continue close relations between parents and children for the whole life. On the one hand, this need is conditioned by the transmission of culture from one generation to another; on the other by the need of life-long endurance of bonds which form the pattern and starting-point for all social organization. The family is the biological grouping to which all kinship is invariably referred and which determines by rules of descent and inheritance the social status of the offspring. As can be seen, this relation never becomes irrelevant to a man and has constantly to be kept alive. Culture, then, creates a new type of human bond (*un lien nouveau, purement humain*) for which there is no prototype in the animal kingdom. [Differences] not in the ends but in the means by which the ends were reached. . . . Thus culture does not lead man into any direction divergent from the courses of nature. Man still has to court his prospective mate . . . The woman still has to bear and the man to remain with her as guardian. . . . But in all this an astounding variety (*modalites infinies*) of patterns replaces in human societies the one fixed type imposed by instinctive endowment upon all the individuals of a single animal species. The direct response of instinct is replaced by traditional norms. Custom, law, moral rule, ritual, and religious value enter into all the stages of love-making and parenthood.[36]

On first reading, it is not immediately clear how this passage answers the question implicit in the title Deleuze tacked on to it—how *does* an institution satisfy a tendency?—but on second reading, this passage proves to be a dramatic example of what is at stake in the theory of the institution. While the word "tendency" is not present anywhere in the excerpt, Deleuze's translation of Malinowski's "the signal for courtship" as "*le besoin du rapprochement sexuel*" indicates what he had in mind. In apes, when the signal for courtship is triggered, there is an "automatic physiological mechanism," an "instinct," which provides a "direct response" to the desire. In humans, the institution intervenes between the signal and the satisfaction and disrupts the direct response of instinct. It is not that there is not a physiological mechanism at the foundation of our need to mate, Malinowski says, it's that between desire and satisfaction a "complex *dispositif*" intervenes.

This concept of the *dispositif*, then, is what answers Deleuze's question (how does an institution satisfy a tendency?). A *dispositif* seems to comprise several elements—a set of traditions, customs, and norms—and it seems to operate (chronotopically) at three levels—spatial, temporal, and formal. Thus, while the desire to mate is physiologically triggered, the *dispositif* determines the *way* in which we relate to our mate; it puts "young people" in relations of proximity, shapes the appropriate suggestions and forms the "mental atmosphere" of the people involved. It organizes the time and space in which we live, and organizes our "emotional attitude." These norms and traditions are not at all abstract. They anchor themselves directly in the body, acting "upon the human body and stimulat[ing] *innate reactions.*"

Deleuze's second excerpt loosely develops these lines of thought. He called this section "The two poles of the institution" (ritual and utility are the two poles), and he took the text from *Rite et l'outil* (*The Rite and the Tool*), a book by one of Malinowski's students, Charles Le Coeur. But it is the third selection which significantly develops the theory of the institution, and which I again quote in full. It, too, is from Malinowski.

2 Principal elements of the institution.

Every institution is based on a system of needs, biological or derived, which are rephrased in every culture into a specific doctrine. I propose the term 'charter' as a label for such a doctrine on which an institution is based. . . .

The charter of an institution therefore comprises its real and mythological history, and the statement of ideals, aims and principles of organization and of conduct, which result from this past history or mythology. The charter of the family is to be found in the cultural reformulation of the biological drive of sex and all that it implies physiologically, emotionally, economically and legally. . . .

From our definition of charter as collective purpose it results that such a purpose has to be translated into activities. . . . By personnel we understand not merely the numerical membership of a group, but also the way in which the various members are placed into a hierarchy, the manner in which authority, technical and specialized skills, and the division of tasks are apportioned. . . .

[By norms we designate'] a whole realm of regularized behavior which does not exist in the charter. In an occupational group such as a factory, the charter consists in the rules defining its ownership, its business organization, the various labor laws, and the legal rules concerning the relation between organization, labor and employee. The knowledge of the full rules would go far beyond this, and would force us to enter into the technicalities of the work done and into problems of industrial psychology, into customary divisions of labor and consideration of how the efficiency of work is induced by wage, recreation or other stimuli. . . .

We know, however, that human beings not only organize into a definite co-operative structure, not only obey rules, but that in their cultural activities they have to manipulate some sort of material apparatus or other. Here again we see that in each case the material apparatus can be briefly defined and that it is different for each type of grouping. The family manipulates the house and homestead, the family lands, and the implements of domesticity insofar as it is a group of consumers and producers. . . . The state deals with its territory, with military force, and with public funds. . . .

[E]very group is organized for the satisfaction of one main need. . . . the charter is connected with this function, though it is never identified with it. *The function* of an institution therefore is the satisfaction of the need or needs for which that institution was organized. In other words, the function of an institution is equivalent to the enjoyment of the results of the activity by the group or personnel who performed it.[37]

Malinowski's institutional model is based on the structure of practical rationality. When we act, we determine an end and select the means adequate to achieving that end. It is from this model that Malinowski derives what Deleuze calls, in his title to the selection, "the principal elements of the institution." There are four principal elements: (1) the charter, which specifies the end the institution should accomplish; (2) the personnel who carry out specific acts; (3) the norms which the personnel follow; and (4) the material apparatus (territory, buildings, means of transportation, and so on) which conditions this activity.[38] An institution is a coordinated set of means for achieving a determinate end set out in the institution's charter.

This third excerpt accomplishes a number of things. It formalizes the theory of the institution into compact sections, and thus provides a clearer picture of the *dispositif* operative in the first excerpt by classifying its functioning into four distinct operations. It also brings the question of ends and projects to the foreground again. This was explicit in *Empiricism and Subjectivity*: the task of institution was to project an end which would be capable of coordinating desires. Here, that end is called "a charter." Finally, it reinforces Deleuze's implication in *Experience and Subjectivity* that norms were functions of institutions. Here, norms are immanent to a practice or an institution determined by a determinate end articulated in a charter.

If we wanted to generalize the point of these first three excerpts, we could not do better than Deleuze's claim in his introduction to the volume:

> Every institution imposes a series of models on our bodies, even in its involuntary structures, and offers our intelligence a sort of knowledge, a possibility of foresight as project.[39]

Institutions are micropolitical.[40] They intervene and structure our bodies, imposing their own forms of segmentarity upon us—even down to the level of the body's involuntary structures, its sensory-motor system, or its passivity. At the same time, we need to think of institutions at the level of the molar—that good or bad, political judgments are molar.[41] But these two levels fold into each other. The judgments we make, the charters we form, the ends we determine, and the projects we invent articulate us as we articulate them.

Institution and utility

A fourth thing this third excerpt accomplishes is a separation of "charter" from "function." The charter specifies the specific and explicit end of each institution. "Function" specifies the relation between the institution and need, or what Deleuze called, following Hume and the utilitarians, "utility" in *Empiricism and Subjectivity*.

This question of utility is at the forefront of the second part of the first chapter, which Deleuze called "Institution and Utility." Of the three excerpts which fell under the first section, "Analysis of the Institution," two were by Malinowski and the other by one of his students. All three contain some of the baldest statements of functionalism imaginable[42]—the notion, that is, that "[E]very group is organized for the satisfaction of one main need," and that the function of an institution is the satisfaction of that need, as Malinowski put in the quotation above.

Each of the excerpts in the second part of the first chapter develops a sharp critique of functionalism. Already in *Empiricism and Subjectivity*—that is, before any hint of Malinowski was on the page—Deleuze was concerned to avoid "a 'functionalist' interpretation" of Hume, "on the basis of which society is explained by utility, and the institution by drives (*tendance*) or needs" (ES 46). The question here is not whether society is ultimately a satisfaction of a tendency. It is. This is its very definition. The question is whether or not this formula has any explanatory power.

These criticisms, which Deleuze excerpts from thinkers as diverse as Alain, James Frazer, Hume, and Levi-Strauss, could all be read as variations on a concept Lacan invoked in his characterization of the drive: a tendency is indifferent to its object. As Lacan put it, I could be fucking; I could be talking; if the drive is satisfied by either of these activities, what is the functional difference between them? Because of the generality of a drive, it is incapable of *explaining* the various forms of satisfaction it encounters. Levi-Strauss's criticism of functionalism is one of the most forceful. In a passage which Deleuze excerpts here, Levi-Strauss explains that because functions are universal, they explain everything and therefore nothing. "What interests the anthropologist is not the universality of the function . . . but, rather, the fact that the customs are so varied."[43] The implicit question which arises here, then, is how this or that institution can be explained. The excerpts immediately preceding and following this one are both from Hume, and in *Empiricism and Subjectivity*, in a commentary on these two passages, Deleuze summarized their import for a theory of the institution:

> [T]he institution is a system of means, according to Hume, but these means are oblique and indirect; they do not satisfy the drive without also constraining it at the same time. Take, for example, *one* form of marriage, or *one* system of property. Why *this* system and *this* form? A thousand others, which we find in other times and places, are possible. (ES 47)

We might say that these criticisms of functionalism open up a gap in the theory of the institution. At one point, Deleuze even makes this gap between tendency and its satisfaction the very definition of an institution ("an institution exists when the means by which a drive is satisfied are not determined by the drive itself or by specific characteristics" (47)). But what is most interesting about this gap is that the void which it designates requires that we take recourse to another explanatory instance.

A drive cannot explain the institution any more than an institution clarifies the drive it satisfies. We thus have to introduce a new element to the theory of institutions. Deleuze puts it this way in the preface to *Instincts and Institutions*

> [I]t is not enough to say 'the institution is useful', one must still ask the question: useful for whom? For all those who have needs? Or just a few (the privileged class)? Or only for those who control the institution (the bureaucracy)? One of the most profound sociological tasks consists of seeking out the nature of this other instance, on which the social forms of the satisfaction of tendencies depend. The rituals of civilization? The means of production? (DI 20)

Determining the nature of this other instance is the topic of the third and final section of Deleuze's first chapter—"The Original Order of the Institution."

The original order

The third section of the first chapter is called the "The Original Order of the Institution," and in this section, Deleuze collects a series of passages which provide potential answers to the question posed above. In order to explain an institution, we must have recourse to some other force. There must be another instance which explains it. What is the nature of this force? There are five excerpts in this section, but only four orders, and these orders are indicated in the titles Deleuze gave to each passage: the "moral order" (Kant), the "coercive order" (Freud), the "ritual order" (Eliade), and the "involuntary order" (Plekhanov). Each of these four specifies a determinate end for institutional organization by specifying that other instance in relation to which we might understand the evolution of institutional life. I'll briefly summarize the first, second, and fourth.

The first is from a note early in Kant's "Conjectural Beginning of Human History," in which Kant shows by example the difference between the natural order and the moral order. As an animal, man reaches maturity around 16 or 17, at which point he "literally becomes a man." But, from the point of view of his ability to function in civil society, he might very well be a mere youth. The "civilized condition" thus comes into "unavoidable conflict" with the "human species as an animal species." The eventual solution to this, which we are not likely to reach soon, is "a perfect civil constitution (the uttermost goal of culture);" only this can remove the misery which results from this conflict.[44] The implication is that institutions *ought* to be determined in relation to the ideal of a civil constitution which reconciles man as a "moral species" with man as a "physical species" (to quote Deleuze's allusion to Kant in his Rousseau lecture).[45]

The second, an excerpt from Freud's *The Future of an Illusion*, which is meant to illuminate what Deleuze calls the "coercive order," follows from Freud's claim that "civilization has to be defended." Freud begins with an assertion he had developed in *Civilization and its Discontents*: society must be defended because "there are present in all men destructive, and therefore anti-social and anti-cultural" impulses.[46] Individuals feel "as a heavy burden the sacrifices which civilization expects of them in order to make communal life possible." As a consequence, the basic "regulations, institutions, and demands" of society must all be directed to ensure that "men's hostile impulses" do not destroy our fragile society. In a passage which Deleuze did not quote (but which is between two that he did), Freud spells out the ideal of society and its reality.

> One would think that a re-ordering of human relations should be possible, which would remove the sources of dissatisfaction with civilization by renouncing coercion and the suppression of the instincts, so that, undisturbed by internal discord, men might devote themselves to the acquisition of wealth and its enjoyment. That would be the golden age, but it is questionable if such a state of affairs can be realized. It seems rather that every civilization must be built up on coercion and renunciation of instinct.[47]

Freud articulates an ideal here which recalls Kant's ideal constitution: we await that constitution which aligns our desires with our institutions. But if this is the "coercive" order and not the "moral' order," it is because Freud positions himself in the present. We currently lack this constitution, and as a consequence, institutions must impose their order in order to keep hostile forces in check.

The fourth excerpt is from Plekhanov's *The Fundamental Problems of Marxism*. In it Plekhanov asks us to imagine a group of men hunting an elephant. These hunters have a collective end: to kill the elephant. This end is determined by the "wants of the human organism"—the "need for food"—and the means of accomplishing this end are determined by the "conditions of the chase" or what Malinowski would call "the material apparatus." From this arrangement, Plekhanov argues, a certain assemblage of social relations can be understood as a function of need. But we can go further. "We can demand an explanation of the reason *why* men, in seeking to satisfy their wants—for instance, the need for food—sometimes enter into certain kinds of mutual relations, and sometimes into quite other kinds." Plekhanov gives the following answer: "*Sociology*—in the person of Marx—*explains this circumstance as the outcome of the state of their productive forces*." And what this ultimately means is that we have to understand "the appearance of aims in social man (social 'teleology'), as a necessary consequence of a social process ultimately determined by the course of economic development." If this is an "involuntary" order, it is not because it refers to our passivity, but because it refers institutions to a force over which we have no control: the course of economic development.

The fact that this last order appears as one among many possible ways of explaining the nature and destination of institutional organization suggests that Deleuze puts Marxism—or a certain interpretation of Marx—on the same level as Freud, Kant, and Eliade's accounts of ritual. He does not seem to grant any of these orders an explanatory priority. And we might tie this back to *Empiricism and Subjectivity*. He argued there that in order to explain the institution, we ultimately have to take recourse to "circumstance."

Imagination is revealed as a veritable production of extremely diverse *models*: when drives (*les tendances*) are reflected in an imagination submitted to the principles of association, institutions are determined by the figures traced by the drives according to the circumstances. (ES 48)

This is a complex sentence, but the basic idea is this. An institution is the reflection of tendency in and by the imagination. But the imagination invents models as a function of circumstance—models which ultimately redirect a drive in relation to circumstance. The model or general rule which the imagination produces is always referred to a contingent outside, and it is this relation which explains the institution, not the relation of utility: "the drive does not explain the institution; what explains it is the *reflection of the drive in the imagination*," where this reflection is determined by the accidents of a contingent "circumstance." Put differently, this third instance cannot be determined philosophically, but only empirically.

This, however, does not exhaust Deleuze's discussion of the original order of the institution. To close the chapter, Deleuze provides an excerpt from Groethuysen's *Le Libéralisme de Montesquieu*. Unlike the other excerpts, this one is not treated as an "order." Instead, Deleuze gives the selection the following title: "The Political End (*finalité*) of Institutions: Security or Liberty?" This is not a question Groethuysen raises in the passage. It is one Deleuze expects the passage to answer, and the answer is unequivocal. The Hobbsian response—security—makes only the briefest of appearances in the excerpt. It is rather the Rousseauean—or Spinozan—answer which is dominant: the end of an institution is freedom, and the basic question of the passage is how "active" freedom is achieved.[48] There are a couple of ways to read this, but I think the most straightforward is to see this as a reappearance of Deleuze's ethics at the level of the political. There is no way to determine in advance those forces which lead to the creation of an institution. They could be moral, ritual, economic, or coercive. But once the institution is in existence, we can specify its end: freedom.

We can summarize this account of the institution into three provisional propositions, each of which would require considerably more development. First, institutions function by simultaneously imposing "a series of models on our bodies, even in its involuntary structures" and by offering our "intelligence a sort of knowledge, a possibility of foresight as project." They perform *a certain articulation* of the sensible the thinkable and the actable which takes place on both molar and molecular registers. Second, it is impossible to determine in advance why *this* system or *this* form. Each institution is a node in a network which responds to multiple orders at once. Institutions are always explained by another instance, but this instance is not capable of being determined philosophically. But, finally, we can say those institutions are good which increase our power of activity and thus carry us forward to our power of activity. We, thus, rediscover (and with all the problems such a discovery entails) Deleuze's ethical perfectionism at the level of the political.

Later Deleuze

I began my discussion of *Instincts and Institutions* by taking issue with the narrative of Deleuze's itinerary which claims that the 60s represent an entirely new Deleuze, and that it is this Deleuze which provides the foundations of the work most people find interesting—namely the major texts of the 70s, 80s, and early 90s. I'd like to now return to this question and try to show that Deleuze's later work develops not only the ideas of the major texts of the 60s, but also the major claims of *Empiricism and Subjectivity* and *Instincts and Institutions* with respect to the question of institutions. In *Deleuze's Hume*, Jeff Bell has already gone a long way in this direction by making important connections between *Empiricism and Subjectivity* and Deleuze's later texts, with particular attention to the way in which the theory of the institution helps us think through the theory of the assemblage in *A Thousand Plateaus*.[49] I'd like to strengthen these connections by focusing on the most basic structure of *Anti-Oedipus*.[50] Despite the book's immense complexity, the conceptual schema which it works through is more or less readily graspable: at its core, the book is an account of how desiring-production relates to social production.

The first important connection we can make with the theory of the institution is in coming to terms with what Deleuze and Guattari mean by desiring-production. The concept is one we have already encountered under several different names. Desiring-production is a genetic process which takes as its point of departure the Deleuzian state of nature: partial objects in a state of dispersion.[51] In this state, there is a passive self—the body without organs—which carries out a series of syntheses on these partial objects, the very molecules of the molecular. Desiring-production is the process by which this passive self takes up partial objects and in the course of a progressive synthesis develops itself. "Desire is the set of *passive syntheses* that engineer partial objects . . . ."[52] "Desiring-machine" is the name Deleuze and Guattari give to the assemblage of three passive syntheses.

If we want to connect *Anti-Oedipus* with the Deleuze of the 50s, we could characterize each of these syntheses as a *tendency*, and desiring-production as a whole as a certain assemblage of tendencies. This is not as far-off as it sounds. There were, I argued above, at least two contextual meanings we could attribute to the concept of tendency as it functioned in *Instincts and Institutions*: tendency as drive and tendency as duration or time. One of the central tasks of *Difference and Repetition* was to elide these two points of view. In the second chapter of that book, the three passive syntheses were shown to be both constitutive of time *and* explainable in the psychoanalytic vocabulary of drives (this latter argument was prepared by Deleuze's arguments in *Coldness and Cruelty* that the drives articulated in Freud's metapsychology ought to be understood as properly transcendental[53]).[54] This would lead us to read the process of time-constitution as it is accomplished by the three passive syntheses in *Difference and Repetition* as a development of Deleuze's early discussion of tendency.[55] From here, it is only a small step to *Anti-Oedipus* which fully takes up the theory of passive synthesis articulated in *Difference and Repetition* and *The Logic of Sense*.[56]

If we accept that the process of desiring-production is the significantly developed but functionally equivalent notion of the 1953 theory of tendencies, this raises the question as to what happens to the theory of the institution. The institution was defined as the indirect and social satisfaction of tendency, and it functioned by determining an end which was capable of "reflecting" desire. This is, I want to argue, how social production works in *Anti-Oedipus*. The theory of the institution is what lets us grasp the conceptual core of *Anti-Oedipus*, the relation between desiring-production and social production.

As Deleuze and Guattari put it, social formations are nothing more than desiring-machines under "determinate conditions." They are an assemblage of tendencies under institutional reflection.

> By 'determinate conditions' we mean those statistical forms into which the machines enter as so many stable forms, unifying, structuring, and proceeding by means of large heavy aggregates; the selective pressures that group the parts retain some of them and exclude others, organizing the crowds. These are, therefore, the same machines, but not at all the same regime, the same relationship, the same magnitude, or the same use of the syntheses.[57]

The connection between desiring-production and social production, then, is made by bringing desire, or the passives syntheses, under "so many stable forms." These forms unify, structure and exert selective pressures on desiring-machines. Social forms, Deleuze and Guattari argue, are "institutions of desire." It is necessary to discover, they say early in the text,

> how social production and relations of production are an institution of desire, how affects or drives (*pulsions*) form part of the infrastructure itself. For *they are part of it, they are present there in every way* while creating within the economic forms their own repression, as well as the means for breaking this repression.[58]

We might read this passage as adding a lower level to the infrastructure. Below production and the relations of production lie machinic processes (Deleuze and Guattari describe things this way themselves in *A Thousand Plateaus*[59]). Production and the relations of production organize desire and coordinate the drives. They create institutions of desire. Or, to use the language of later Deleuze and Guattari, they create assemblages.[60]

This particular passage of *Anti-Oedipus* is a brief commentary on the work of Pierre Klossowski, and in a footnote, Deleuze and Guattari encourage us look more closely at "Klossowski's meditation on the relationship between drives (*pulsions*) and institutions."[61] They cite two texts: Klossowski's essay, "Sade et Fourier," and *Nietzsche and the Vicious Circle*. In this latter text, Klossowski develops a theory of the institution which is functionally equivalent to the one developed in *Empiricism and Subjectivity* and *Instincts and Institutions*. This is not the place to make this argument in any detail, but I can quickly sketch its outline. The most basic level of subjectivity for Klossowski is that of the impulses, a teeming flux of "drives" and "intensities." The satisfaction of these drives results in "phantasms." These two elements taken together constitute Klossowski's original position: "Nothing exists apart from *impulses* that are essentially generative of *phantasms*."[62] Such a world, however, is essentially chaotic, and in it, our continued existence remains uncertain. The only way out of this situation is, as in Deleuze's Hume, invention—"existence is sustained only through fabulation."[63] The product of this fabulation is what Klossowski calls a "simulacrum," an image or *model* which represents a goal and gives our life meaning.

> *To fix a goal, to give a meaning*—not merely to orient living forces but also to elicit *new centers of forces*: this is what the simulacrum does: a simulacrum of a goal, a simulacrum of meaning—*which must be invented!*[64]

We can extract several important points from this short passage, all of which resonate with the theory of the institution in *Empiricism and Subjectivity* and *Instincts and Institutions*. The first is that this goal and this meaning must be invented or fabulated. Second, while the institution is always artificial, it functions by reflecting tendency. It "orients living forces." It organizes the drives, and, to borrow a locution from another of Klossowski's texts, it brings about a "precarious armistice"[65] among these drives. Third, in coordinating our drives by fixing them on a goal, our existence takes on a meaning in the sense that our desires and actions acquire determinate ends. Finally, for Klossowski, this orientation of living forces is not a closed process. Institution "orient living forces," but they also open up an entirely new horizon on which we can discover "new centers of forces" and enter into new possibilities for life. We thus find in Klossowski the basic elements of the much younger Deleuze's theory of the institution.

The pivot around which the conceptual structure of *Anti-Oedipus* turns, then, was laid out in Deleuze's foundational texts of 1953. In the same way that institutions organize and redirect tendencies, social formations impose unifying, structuring, and stabilizing relations upon desire. Deleuze's formulation of the central idea of *Instincts and Institutions* works equally well for *Anti-Oedipus*: "Every institution imposes a series of models on our bodies, even in its involuntary structures, and offers our intelligence a sort of knowledge, a possibility of foresight as project."[66]

There is one final point worth making here. Not only is it the case that Deleuze maintains a strong relationship between tendency and institution, desire and social formation, but he still insists that this relationship cannot be explained functionally. Throughout *Anti-Oedipus* we find passages which echo the antifunctionalist arguments of *Empiricism and Subjectivity* and *Instincts and Institutions*. To cite only one example:

> It has often been said and demonstrated that an institution cannot be explained by its use, any more than an organ can. Biological formations and social formation are not formed in the same way in which they function. Nor is there a biological, sociological, linguistic, etc., functionalism at the level of large determinate aggregates.[67]

This repudiation of "molar functionalism" explains two statements which seem, at a first glance to be contradictory: (1) *Anti-Oedipus* is "from beginning to end a book of political philosophy;"[68] (2) "No political program will be elaborated within the framework of schizoanalysis."[69] The apparent contradiction turns on the word "program:" *Anti-Oedipus* provides a descriptive, but not a normative political philosophy. If this is related to the question of functionalism, it is because in the same way that institutions had to be explained by another instance—an instance which was not grounded philosophically—the theory of assemblages finds its determination outside of itself. There is no political program. "Universal history," Deleuze and Guattari say, has no direction. Are there not, then, any criteria we can derive from this system which would allow us to distinguish good from bad institutions? I think there are, but to do that we have to turn from an attention to the aesthetics of these systems to the question of ethics.

Norms...

Anti-Oedipus is exclusively concerned with the negative or oppressive nature of institutions. Institutions work by "snaring the unconscious," "crushing the whole of desire-production, replacing it with a system of beliefs."[70] The "goal of schizoanalysis" is to understand Spinoza's basic question—how is it that we desire our own oppression—and one answer to this question seems to be that we do so by forming institutions—*any* institution. Thus, the only way out is to regress from the molar back to the molecular. While this may be useful analytically, it does not provide us with any direction when it comes to creating institutions. We might say that for Deleuze, as for Rawls, "the most important natural duty" is "to support and to further just institutions,"[71] but unlike Rawls, Deleuze never seems to say what might constitute a just institution.

This question has recently been taken up in several important studies of Deleuze's political philosophy, and it has been given a variety of answers. Paul Patton has persuasively argued that "the overriding norm [for Deleuze] is that of deterritorialization."[72] Todd May has identified two implicit normative principles structuring Deleuze's thought: the antirepresentationalist principle (we ought to avoid representing others as much as possible) and the principle of difference (we should make as much room as possible for alternate practices and ways of doing things).[73] And Roberto Esposito has recently argued for what he calls a "norm of life"—a norm which does not come from above but which draws its power from "the immanent impulse of life" and which participates in the "potentiality of life's becoming."[74] Each of these arguments, in and of itself, is persuasive, but it remains unclear how they work together. What I want to suggest in closing is that there is indeed a systematic unity to these principles and that this unity is best seen from the perspective of Deleuze's early theory of the institution.

It is worth emphasizing at the start, however, that this argument is burdened by two immediate difficulties. First, as Ian Buchanan has recently argued, this attempt to uncover a set of consistent normative principles is very often accompanied by a seductive "category mistake."[75] Deleuze's texts are laden with value judgments. As I argued in the first chapter above, this is often the only way we find our orientation on a first reading of his texts: immanence is good, transcendence is bad; trees are bad, rhizomes are good. This whole series of evaluations, however, is usually implicit. It's never entirely clear why a rhizome is better than a tree, or at what register this evaluation is legitimate. It's not that we could not come up with an answer, and probably a good one. The problem is that the point of view from which Deleuze is speaking, or the end toward which he is aiming, is not at all clear. And this is what leads to the category mistake: it is all too easy to take the set of values structuring Deleuze's texts and transpose them to the level of the ontological the ethical or the political.

This question is further complicated by its tendency to ignore one of the most general principles of Deleuze's thought. Any attempt to articulate a determinate end of action or organization seems to be grounded on a prior refusal to acknowledge that Deleuze's philosophy is essentially non-teleological. It never speaks in advance to the ends of humanity or to the ends of whatever replaces humanity because the essence of the thought is creative. We do not know what is possible and we do not know what we can do in advance. What we can become is a permanently open question. But despite these difficulties, Deleuze's early writings on institutions already make important gestures in the direction of a coherent set of normative principles.

In *Empiricism and Subjectivity*, Deleuze made three important moves with respect to this question: (1) he identified norms or rules not with a pre-given set of ends but with the active determination of ends; (2) he entrusted the act by which we determine ends to the inventive capacity of human nature (the central task of institution is setting an end or "fixing a goal," to quote Klossowski); but crucially, (3) he insisted that these norms are set and these ends are fixed always as a function of the relationship between "tendency" and circumstance.[76] Normative principles always refer to a third explanatory instance which remains outside of philosophical determination because our needs and circumstances change (and our response to our needs and circumstances create new needs and desires, thus permanently altering the "objective situation"). The task of thought is to respond to new situations and develop new strategies for dealing with these contingent encounters and the needs they create.

In other words, the set of normative principles in the theory of the institution takes its coherence from the ontological subject at the foundation of Deleuze's ethics, aesthetics, and (I am arguing) politics. And if we push this only a little further, we can say that certain principles can be derived from each of its three levels: primary organization, or passivity; secondary organization or creative thought; and the molar, tertiary organization or representational thought.[77] In relation to our passivity, we can say that those institutions are good which contribute to our becoming active. From the heart of the system, thought or virtuality, we can derive Esposito's norm of life, and, as a corollary, May's principle of difference: those institutions are good which provide creative responses to the state of affairs from which they arose. And from the point of view of molar existence, we can say that those institutions are good which maintain a constant connection to the state of affairs from which they arose (the tendency of representations to fall into clichés and dead representations—and thus into an illegitimate use of representation (see Chapter 2 above)—is, I would argue, what grounds deterritorialization as the overriding norm). What I am proposing, then, is that Deleuze provides us with the following normative criteria: institutions should liberate us from our passivity and prevent our activity from becoming ossified.

Notes

Chapter 1

1. Blanchot, "Literature and the Right to Death" 310.
2. Bergson, *Creative Evolution* p. 158.
3. NP 104.
4. DR 167.
5. DR 131/171; original emphasis, trans. modified.
6. PS 93. Deleuze's emphasis on this postulate will remain constant all the way to his last major text, *What is Philosophy?*, Cf. WP 61.
7. PS 94–5.
8. DR 131.
9. NP 103.
10. WP 144.
11. PS 94.
12. PS 94.
13. Cressole 103.
14. NG 6.
15. This is Macherey's strategy in 'The Encounter', p. 149.
16. Foucault, 'Theatriculm Phiosophicum' p. 196.
17. WP 83.
18. CII 222.
19. *Friendship*, 173.
20. On the importance of *Critique* for the major figures of Deleuze's generation, see Patron, pp. 154–62.
21. The importance of the review form for twentieth-century French thought is still massively understudied. The most substantial study to date is Eleanor Kaufman's *The Delirium of Praise*. Kaufman has shown the extent to which such a form allowed these thinkers to realize in their prose style the very philosophical concepts and themes they put forward in their own writing: it opens up a space

of impersonality, it pathologizes thought and incorporealizes matter, it destabilizes relations between the normal and the pathological, and above all the encounter with a concept does not happen in a blue sky of ideas but in an encounter with publications or concrete events. I want to draw a far less sophisticated conclusion—and one I hope is obvious to the point of appearing banal: the conventions of clear and direct prose that we assume in our major reviews are not operative in many of the central texts of this period.

22 Surya 369.
23 "Editorial." *Critique* (June 1946) 1: p. 2. As Philippe Roger notes, this was one of the most distinct characteristics of the journal, "among the journals of the day . . . polemic and demolition were laws of the genre" (Roger, 695). This comes across well in an interesting letter in which Derrida rejects an unnamed text for publication. Derrida explains that its "polemic tone" is the "tone of the *Times Literary Supplement* or of American or English criticism" and would detract from the seriousness of the article's "analyses" (quoted in Patron, 98). This captures another aspect of Deleuze's style that I will not discuss here, and that's his own rejection of polemic.
24 Surya 369.
25 Patron 360.
26 DR 76.
27 DR 82.
28 DR 93/125; translation modified.
29 EP 275–6.
30 EP 292.
31 Leibniz lectur 04/15/1980.
32 Badiou, *Deleuze* 15; original emphasis. Cf. *Theoretical Writings*, Chapter 6.
33 Much of the difficulty of Deleuze's chapter comes from his attempt to show how these faculties are not already there, as I'm suggesting for ease in exposition, but are actually produced in the act of synthesis itself.
34 DR 96–7.
35 DR 109.
36 DR 101–2.
37 DR 118.
38 The one exception is DR 118, but this is hardly helpful.
39 This example from *Difference and Repetition* is illustrative even here. Despite the fact that the first account of passive synthesis was made in the language of faculty psychology, very few of

Deleuze's readers have connected this account of synthesis in Chapter 2 with the faculty psychology of Chapter 3.
40 ATP 311.
41 ATP 311.
42 ATP 311.
43 ATP 311.
44 KA 70.
45 KA 70.
46 ATP 23.
47 ATP 25.
48 C2 147.
49 KA 20.
50 C2 129.
51 DG 117.
52 Deleuze's thesis advisor Georges Canguilhelm developed a similar argument across the second chapter of *Knowledge of Life* arguing simultaneously that in the development of cell theory, biology borrowed concepts from other fields as disparate as geometry and political science *and* that this is not illegitimate.
53 This is not to say that the descriptions do not change with the function. In *Difference and Repetition*, multiplicities are ideal and 'singularity' is a mathematical metaphor. In *Anti-Oedipus*, there is an obvious reversal: multiplicities are material and 'singularity' is used in its traditional philosophical sense to refer to the immediate object of intuition.
54 Macherey 144.
55 Bergson, *Creative Evolution* p. 158.
56 Delanda 202.
57 DR 8.

Chapter 2

1 CE 126.
2 LS 218; original emphasis.
3 Kerslake, *Immanence and the Vertigo of Philosophy*, p. 5.
4 DR 87.
5 For an excellent discussion of Deleuze's Proust from a Kantian point of view, see Anne Sauvagnargues, Chapter 4.

6   See Chapter 3, below.
7   The text that Deleuze is alluding to here is Merleau-Ponty's introduction to *Les Philosophes célèbres*, an anthology which Merleau-Ponty organized and to which Deleuze contributed his essay "Bergson, 1859–1941" in *Desert Islands*.
8   Leibniz lecture, 4/22/1980.
9   Leibniz lecture, 5/20/1980.
10 EP 28.
11 EP 11.
12 WP 60.
13 See Hallward and Badiou.
14 CPR Bxvi.
15 Leibniz lecture, 5/20/1980.
16 Leibniz lecture, 5/20/1980.
17 *What is Grounding?*; my emphasis.
18 Meillassoux, *After Finitude* p. 63, 7.
19 This translation is Christian Kerslake's. See *Immanence* p. 16.
20 NP 52.
21 NP 51; Foucault makes an almost identical move in his *Introduction to Kant's* Anthropology, pp. 66–8. This is because Foucault is trying to do from within limits of Kant's *oeuvre* what Deleuze does from the outside: fold the transcendental back into the empirical.
22 DR 87; Cf. FC 60.
23 See Makkreel, Chapter 2, for a good overview of this.
24 DR 87.
25 DR 87.
26 Merleau-Ponty, *Phenomenology of Perception* pp. 268–70.
27 DR 91.
28 The final sections of *What is Grounding?* are very illuminating from this point of view. For a good overview in English, see Kerslake, *Vertigo*, Chapter 1.
29 KCP 62; original emphasis.
30 NP 50.
31 NP 50.
32 DR 96.
33 NP 51–2.
34 NP 101.

35 NP 101; my emphasis.
36 See, in particular, KCP 18 and his Kant lecture on 4/4/1978.
37 "All Bergson asks for are movements and intervals between movements which serve as units" (C1 61).
38 WP, EPXXX.
39 See Philippa Rothfield's "Dance and the Passing Moment" for an illuminating discussion of the relation between force, the body, and time.
40 This conception of the finitude of synthesis is taken directly from Kant. See KCP 50.
41 ATP 311; cf. WP 180.
42 NP 91.
43 FB 93–4.
44 WP 128.
45 CJ§26 V.258.
46 CJ§26 V.254.
47 CJ§26 V.254.
48 CJ§26 V.258; original emphasis.
49 Kant seminar (04/04/1978).
50 *Groundwork* p. 73.
51 Kant, *Critique of Practical Reason* p. 15.
52 CPr 45; my emphasis. See *Groundwork* p. 113.
53 CPr 57.
54 CPr 33.
55 I develop this in Chapter 3 below.
56 WP 57.
57 For a lucid description of the mechanics of formal reflection, see Walter Benjamin, *The Concept of Criticism in German Romanticism*, pp. 120–6.
58 This is clearest in *The Logic of Sense* where Deleuze writes that the aleatory point "returns to its beginning which remained external to it (castration); but to the extent that beginning itself was a result, [it] also returns to that from which the beginning had resulted [the system of the passive self]; and finally, little by little, it returns to the absolute origin from which everything proceeds (the depths [or what I have called the material field]). LS 219.
59 This is the basis of Deleuze's distinction between *chronos*, the present of the passive self, and *aion*, the time without present occupied by the aleatory point. (LS 162, 165).

60 If it's role has not yet been noticed here, it is because "*aléatoire*" has been translated as "uncertain"C2 175/228; for differential relations, C2 179, and for categories of problems or of life, C2 186 and 189. I develop this reading of the cinema books in Chapter 4.

61 Here, Deleuze speaks of 'that transcendent "aleatory point," always Other by nature, in which all the essences are enveloped like so many differentials of thought, and which signifies the highest power of thought only by virtue of also designating the unthinkable or the inability to think at the empirical level" (DR 144).

62 CE 354; For a lucid account of this, see Paola Marrati's *Cinema and Philosophy*, Chapters 1 and 3.

63 CE 50.

64 CE 103.

65 CE 51.

66 CE 89; my de-emphasis.

67 CE 54.

68 CE 54.

69 See CE 126–9; 354.

70 BG 112.

71 LS 171.

72 Leibniz lecture, 5/20/1980.

73 There is a (post-)Kantian reading of this as well. At the end of his *Introduction to Kant's* Anthropology, Foucault asks whether Nietzsche had not already shown us that the death of man implied the death of God. If this is the case, it would reverse the classical relation between the finite and the infinite. This would show that 'finitude is not an end but rather that camber and knot in time when the end is the beginning" (Foucault 124).

74 DI 37.

75 DI 38.

76 KCP 59.

77 KCP 18; original emphasis.

78 WP 56.

79 See Longuenesse, p. 116 for the short version; Chapter 9 for the detailed version.

80 KCP 62; original emphasis.

81 DR 218.

82 DR 219; my emphasis.

83 LS 76; he had already made this point in *Difference and Repetition* (DR 36).
84 DR 226.
85 DR 226.
86 DR 98.
87 See Chapter 5 of my *Deleuze and the Genesis of Representation* for an extended version of this argument.
88 DR 266.
89 DR 279, "the resonances between series put ideal relations into play." This is a complex passage, and the point I want it to make is not immediately clear. "Resonances" is one formulation of the second passive synthesis. "Ideal relations" are one component of the Idea. What I understand Deleuze to be saying here, then, is that in its active form, the second synthesis (resonance) does its work according to the role given to it by the Idea, and specifically according to "ideal relations" (as opposed to singularities). Elsewhere, he tells us that when actualized, ideal relations determine quality. Common sense is a "qualitative synthesis," and it, therefore, seems to be based on the second synthesis of time which, in its active form, incarnates ideal relations.
90 DR 226.
91 Klossowski, *Such a Deathly Desire* p. 109.
92 DR 98.
93 DI 96.
94 DR 235.
95 DR 281.
96 LS 146; my emphasis.
97 FB, Chapter 11.

Chapter 3

1 EP 262.
2 Spinoza, *Ethics* III.da.2.
3 In this, and in much of what follows, I am indebted to Stanley Cavell's work on perfectionism, and in particular, on *Conditions Handsome and Unhandsome*. Deleuze, I will imply below, relates more or less directly to numbers 6–8, 10–12, and 28 on Cavell's list. Cavell 6–7.
4 EP 11.

5 An earlier version of this section of the chapter was published as "Form, Plasticity and Passivity" in MonoKL's *International Gilles Deleuze Issue* (11–12), Spring 2012. I am grateful to Vokan Çelebi for allowing me to develop it here.
6 EP 219, 221.
7 EP 262.
8 EP 209.
9 EP 278.
10 EP 278.
11 EP 222.
12 EP 218.
13 EP 217.
14 EP 239; Deleuze is clear, however, that these affections are not contingent. They are, in fact, governed by natural laws. But from the point of view of the body, subject to the play of these laws, everything seems to happen as if by chance. Spinoza can call this order "fortuitous" (*fortuitus occursus*) without thereby introducing the least contingency. For, the order of encounters is itself perfectly determinate: its necessity is that of extensive parts and their external determination *ad infinitum*. But it is fortuitous in relation to the order of relations. (EP 238).
15 EP 219.
16 LS 5–6.
17 Sean Bowden is very good on this. See Priority, Chapter 5.
18 NP 50.
19 EP 225.
20 EP 226.
21 EP 219.
22 See Kinser, Chapter 4 for a strong account of Spinoza's perfectionism. He argues persuasively that "Spinoza does not regard freedom as valuable because it is a condition for our agency. Rather, he argues that freedom and autonomy are important because they are constitutive of our flourishing" (86).
23 EP 274.
24 EP 283.
25 EP 289.
26 EP 240–1.
27 EP 295.
28 EP 243.

29 EP 289; my emphasis.
30 EP 246; original emphasis. Deleuze makes a nearly identical argument in *Nietzsche and Philosophy*, p. 114.
31 EP 220.
32 EP 220.
33 EP 220; original emphasis.
34 EP 311.
35 EP 280.
36 EP 279.
37 SPP 55.
38 EP 294.
39 EP 297.
40 Kant, *Critique of Pure Reason* p. A311/B367.
41 EP 299.
42 EP 301.
43 EP 280; my emphasis.
44 EP 285. Deleuze is quoting Spinoza here. *Ethics* V.10p.
45 EP 296.
46 EP 296; my emphasis.
47 SPP 58.
48 It is true that Spinoza uses the same verb in the proposition under question, but the context is completely different. V.10s.
49 See Deleuze's discussion of this in KCP 25 and 59.
50 DR 214; translation modified.
51 See Ibid. 170–7. Cf. my *Difference and Repetition* 147–8.
52 An earlier version of these arguemnts appeared in my essay "Beleiving in the World." I am grateful to EUP for allowing me to use them here.
53 NP 39–40, cf. 62.
54 NP 40.
55 NP 62.
56 NP 63.
57 NP 50.
58 NP 50.
59 NP 85: "The genetic element (power) determined the relation of force wit force and qualifies related forces. As plastic element, it simultaneously determines and is determined, simultaneously qualifies and is qualifies."

60 NP 52.
61 NP 112–14.
62 NP 112–13.
63 NP 48, 50.
64 NP 63.
65 These two only come together in an extremely complicated way in the final sections of Deleuze's text, and *Nietzsche and Philosophy* is arguably best read as an attempt to solve this very problem which bothered Kant during the last few years of his life and which occupies several important passages in his *Opus postumum*. The *Opus postumum* ends with the claim that *"Zoroaster"* represents "philosophy in the whole of its complex, comprehended under a principle" and thus completes the synthesis of the practical philosophy and theoretical philosophy (Kant, *Opus* 255). For Deleuze, it is not Zarathustra who accomplishes this, but Dionysus.
66 NP 48.
67 NP 50.
68 NP 91; my emphasis.
69 NP 70.
70 This is especially clear in *Cinema 1*.
71 Bryant, 'Ethics' 26.
72 Bryant, 'Ethics' 27.
73 NP 68; my understanding of this moment in Deleuze's text was greatly improved by Sanja Dejanovic's paper, "The Creative Power of Desire: A Brief Genealogy from Kant to Deleuze."
74 NP 68.
75 NP 69.
76 NP 69; Deleuze returned to this formulation almost 20 years later in a lecture on Spinoza (Spinoza lecture 9/12/1980).
77 NP 68; original emphasis.
78 LS 143–7.
79 This is the basic sense of the concept of counteractualization in *The Logic of Sense*. See my discussion of this below pn p. XXX.
80 NP 69.
81 NP 103.
82 NP 71.
83 NP 97.
84 NP 101.
85 NP 100.

86 KCP 69.
87 NP 100; Not only does Deleuze explicitly link this claim to Kant here, but much of what Deleuze writes in these passages reappears in his characterization of the Copernican Revolution in *Kant's Critical Philosophy*. See KCP 14; Cf. NP 91–2 and 100.
88 NP 101.
89 NP 101.
90 Bergson, MM 150.
91 NP 101.
92 NP 103; original emphasis.
93 See, in particular, SPP 22–5.
94 EP 261–2.
95 EP 262.
96 Rawls' criticism of perfectionism in *A Theory of Justice* (§50) turns on a confusion of culture as a set of art works and culture as the cultivation of our powers which those works may or may not achieve. In other words, Rawls elevates the means to the end.
97 *Ethics* III.11.s, for example, defines joy as a *passion* which moves the mind toward greater perfection.
98 Macherey 157.
99 Sean Bowden is especially clear on how this works in *The Logic of Sense*. Bowden, *Priority*, pp. 207–8. Cf. CC 111–21.
100 DI 21.
101 NP 163, 168–9.
102 NP 169.
103 NP 94.
104 Cavell 9.

Chapter 4

1 NP 102.
2 WP 191; Cf. KCP 47, "The essential thing is the design, the composition . . . ."
3 WP 164.
4 ATP 316.
5 EP 262.
6 Badiou, *Deleuze* p. 15.

7 An earlier version of these arguemnts appeared in my essay "Beleiving in the World." I am grateful to EUP for allowing me to use it here.
8 C1 58, original emphasis. Deleuze downplays Bergson's claim that images on the plane of immanence are regulated by the laws of nature. Bergson: "Here I am in the presence of images, in the vaguest sense of the word, images perceived when my senses are open to them, unperceived when they are closed. All these images act and react upon one another in all their elementary parts according to constant laws which I call laws of nature. . ." (MM 17).
9 Deleuze EP 217. Modal existence is defined in *Expressionism in Philosophy* in the same way the plane of immanence is here: "the nature of extensive parts is such that they 'affect one another' ad infinitum" (EP 217; cf. 201–2).
10 For the drop of wine in the ocean, see Deleuze LS 6; for the discussion of universal cesspools, see LS 187.
11 EP 191–9.
12 Deleuze himself made this analogy (C1 xiv; NG 46–9).
13 Marrati 41.
14 In Kant, recognition is also the synthesis of perception (apprehension) and a passive memory (reproduction). In Bergson, the rule for this synthesis is provided by affection or memory. In Kant, it is supplied by the understanding. My argument below is that in Deleuze, as a result of the permanent crisis in recognition, this rule has to be created. Deleuze assigns this role to Godard, the creator of categories.
15 In *Cinema 2*, Deleuze frequently links "virtuality," "sense," and the time-image. See, for example, C2 99.
16 EP 24.
17 Translation modified. The French reads, "ce point problématique, aléatoire, et pourtant non-arbitraire" (1985: 228). In the current English edition, "aléatoire" has been translated as "uncertain," thus obscuring an important connection between *Cinema 2* and Deleuze's earlier texts.
18 For a more developed version of these arguments, see my "Believing in the World: Toward an Ethics of Form."
19 NP 102. This, too, is as Kantian as it is Nietzschean. See DI 67–8 where Deleuze claims that to get to the bottom of Kant's aesthetics, we must "leave behind the spectator's point of view."
20 In the name of simplicity and clarity I do not discuss here the way in which the advent of the time-image requires a shift from "an aesthetics of the spectator" to an "aesthetics or meta-aesthetics of

the creator"—a move which Deleuze outlined in his reading of Kant and which Deleuze parallels as his own aesthetics approach the Deleuzian equivalent of the Kantian soul (DI 56).

21 DI 69.
22 CJ §1 V.204.
23 CJ §1 and §23 V.244–5.
24 FB 34, 52.
25 Here, again, is the full quotation: pleasure or displeasure "expresses nothing at all in the object but simply a relation to the subject. For this very reason pleasure and displeasure cannot be explained more clearly in themselves; instead, one can only specify what results they have in certain circumstances, so as to make them more recognizable in practice." Kant *Metaphysics of Morals* p. 12.
26 Kant, *Anthropology*, p. 334.
27 EP 240–1. I am not implying that Deleuze was re-writing Spinoza in a Kantian idiom. This definition of pleasure is already in Spinoza (*Ethics* III.Def. of Affects.3.Exp.), and there are good historical reasons for these resonances—namely both Spinoza's and Kant's proximity to a loosely Aristotelian understanding of life, pleasure, and pain. (On this, see Protevi, "Organism as Judgment" and *Political Affect*; Colebrook, *Deleuze and the Meaning of Life*.) I am, rather, pointing to that space of mobility between thinkers which Deleuze set up and in which his thought unfolds.
28 EP 239; 275–6.
29 Here is the full quotation: *Life* is the faculty of a being by which it acts according to the laws of the faculty of desire. The *faculty of desire* is the faculty such a being has of causing, through its ideas, the reality of the objects of these ideas. *Pleasure* is the idea of the agreement of an object or action with the *subjective* conditions of life, that is, with the faculty through which an idea causes the reality of its object (or the direction of the energies of a subject to such an action as will produce the object). CPr 9–10n.
30 The Bloomberg Logic §18 and 19.
31 *Anthropology*, 334.
32 *Anthropology*, 334.
33 Deleuze's own discussion of this is admirably clear. See KCP 46–50, as is Guyer's "The Harmony of the Faculties Revisited" in *Values of Beauty*.
34 CJ §39.
35 CJ §9 V.219.
36 CJ §9 V.219.

37. CJ §9 V.219.
38. CJ §10 V.220.
39. CJ §12 V.222; original emphasis.
40. CJ §12 V.222.
41. For a much more complex view of pleasure, see Gasché 50–1. And Allison (FIND QUOTE).
42. See Gasché, *The Idea of Form* p. 44ff for an excellent discussion of this.
43. Foucault 61.
44. Burke *A Philosophical Enquiry* (80).
45. CJ §29, General Remark, V.277.
46. While it would require considerably more work to make this argument, I suspect that this rejection of indifference is based in Kant's association of the *Gemüt* with the form of inner sense, or time, in *The Critique of Pure Reason* (A33–34/B49–50).
47. CJ §29, General Remark V.277–8; original emphasis. While Foucault does not comment directly on this passage, his discussion of the *Gemüt* (60–6) and the question of the human being in later Kant (73ff.) is an indispensible resource to these passages.
48. See Makkreel Chapter 5 for an illuminating discussion of these passages. He discusses this passage in particular on pp. 104–5.
49. Makkreel helpfully reminds us that this was how Kant characterized the transcendental I in the *Prolegomena*. See Makkreel 105.
50. Gratification, for Kant, is basically corporeal pleasure. See CJ §54, Remark, V.330–1. There is something "animal" about it (V.335).
51. KCP 4.
52. NG 6.
53. CJ §53, Remark V.335; original emphasis. On the notion of the animal, see Makkreel p. 104.
54. Makkreel, 104.
55. KCP 58–61. Deleuze's argument is that "judgment always implies several faculties and expresses the accord between them. . . . [A]ny determinate accord of the faculties . . . presupposes the existence and the possibility of a free indeterminate accord. It is in this free accord that judgment is not only original . . . but manifests the principle of its originality" (58–60).
56. Paul Guyer helpfully points out that the notion of common sense has three distinct meanings: a feeling which is universally communicable; the principle which grounds this universal communicability; and the faculty for judging itself. To avoid the

interpretive problem of selecting one or another of these senses as dominant Guyer argues that each a total explication of one sense implies an account of the other two senses (Guyer, *Claims* 250). While Deleuze is nowhere explicit about this, what I am arguing here is that in his reading of the *Critique of Judgment* common sense functions as a provisional formulation of the faculty of judging which will be subsequently deepened over the course of Kant's text.

57 CJ §11 V.239.
58 CJ §21.
59 CJ §20, §40.
60 CJ §22 V.239.
61 CJ §22 V.240.
62 CJ §26 V.254.
63 CJ §26 V.256.
64 CJ §26 V.254.
65 CJ §28 V.261.
66 CPR A22–3/B37; "Inner sense, by means of which the mind intuits itself, or its inner state, gives, to be sure, no intuition of the soul itself or its inner state."
67 CJ §28 V.261–2.
68 CJ §28 V.262.
69 KCP 51.
70 On this distinction between regulative and genetic principles, see the *Jäsche Logic* §3 p. 92 and CPR A178–9/B221–2.
71 DI 69–70.
72 DI 69; original emphasis.
73 DI 69.
74 CJ §57 V.341. Most Anglo-American critics are hesitant to accept Kant's argument here. See esp. Guyer, *The Claims of Taste* 337–50. Deleuze himself, in fact, is much quieter about this in KCP, though the essential argument is still present.
75 KCP 57; my emphasis.
76 DI 67.
77 KCP 47–8.
78 NP 50.
79 KCP 55.
80 KCP 52 and 55; cf. CJ §28.
81 KCP 56.

82 See my *Deleuze's* Difference and Repetition, pp. 5–10.
83 See Chapter 2 above, p. XXX.
84 KCP 74.
85 Intro 62.
86 DR 69/85.
87 This is admittedly the case only for the essay. In his Kant book, he still raises the question of genesis, but what needs to be produced is the relations between faculties. In the essay based on that chapter, the faculties become "primeval."
88 DI 61.
89 Gasché 57; Cf. Makkreel 95, and Ginsborg, "Lawfulness without a Law."
90 DR 68; for a lucid reading of this passage, see Bryant, *Difference and Giveness*, 98.
91 CJ §26 V.256.
92 DR 68.
93 NP 102.
94 The answer I'm about to provide does not, however, take into account that Deleuze regularly attributes these capacities not just to artists, but to doctors, mathematicians, scientists, philosophers, tennis players, and high jumpers.
95 Marrati 85.
96 Marrati 68.
97 C2 21; my emphasis.
98 Marrati 79.
99 WP 191.
100 WP 164.
101 ATP 316.

Chapter 5

1 ATP 213; original emphasis.
2 ATP 222.
3 DI 21.
4 For this argument, I am greatly indebted to John Protevi's *Political Affect*.
5 See Chapter 2 above.

6 Hardt, *An Apprenticeship*, p. xvii.

7 We might note that this is exactly the strategy of both *Expressionism in Philosophy* (where Deleuze notes that Spinoza was a precursor of Rousseau on these points) and *Empiricism and Subjectivity* with respect to the contract: in both texts, Deleuze provides a brief discussion of the contract and then argues that (to use the language of EP) it is adequate to a rational state but not an actually existing one.

8 These two expressions, "man as a physical species" and man as a "moral species," are not Rousseau's. In the second *Discourse*, Rousseau speaks only of "physical man" and "moral man." They are, rather, Kant's, which he used to characterize moral and physical man in his review of Herder. See below, and *Anthropology, History and Education*, p. 169.

9 *Rousseau* pp. 18–19.

10 Discourse on the Origins of Inequality p. 159.

11 *Rousseau* 10.

12 *Rousseau* p. 10.

13 *Rousseau* p. 10.

14 For example, NP 50.

15 There are, as always, important exceptions to this. See Bell, Clark, and Lambert.

16 "Almost all the governments which exist at present, or of which there remains any record in story, have been founded originally, either on usurpation or conquest, or both, without any presence of a fair consent or voluntary subjection of the people." Hume, *Political Essays*, pp. 189–90.

17 Hume, *Political Essays*, p. 193.

18 Perhaps the best way of putting this is to say that Hume opts for the first contract in Rousseau.

19 It is perhaps worth noting here that this is why, counterintuitively, the connotations of bureaucracy and oppression which the word "institution" usually elicits do not immediately apply to the Deleuzian and Humean notion of the institution: an institution is initially a positive means of satisfaction rather than a negative means of oppression.

20 This was also how he characterized the contract in his Rousseau lecture as well. Rousseau 22.

21 EP 41. On the importance of this assimilation of practical rationality to part-whole relationships more generally, see Vogler, *Reasonably Vicious*.

22 See Broderick's preface to *The French Institutionalists* for a good overview of Hauriou and Georges Renard (who Deleuze also quotes from in I&I).
23 Kerslake, "Desire and the Dialectics of Love," p. 53.
24 [T]he *Trieb* can in no way be limited to a psychological notion. It is an absolutely fundamental ontological notion . . . . Lacan, *Ethics of Psychoanalysis*, 127.
25 Lacan, *Four Fundamental Concepts*, p. 164.
26 168; original emphasis.
27 165–6.
28 Lacan, *The Four Fundamental Concepts*, 168.
29 CE 13; cf. 106.
30 CE 107.
31 CE 107.
32 For a lucid overview, see Valentine Moulard-Leonard's *Bergson-Deleuze Encounters* 58–63.
33 CE 98.
34 CE 99; my emphasis.
35 Deleuze regularly omitted passages without noting it, altered translations, and added passages, usually for the sake of clarity, but not always. His unnoted omissions are marked here by ellipses in brackets . . . and his additions are placed in brackets, [like this]. Where Deleuze's translations significantly depart from the original or have important connotations, I have included his French in italics.
36 Malinowski, *Sex and Repression in Savage Society*, pp. 153–75.
37 Malinowski, *Freedom and Civilization*, pp. 157–64.
38 Most institutional theorists keep this basic structure, but add sanctions. See, for example, Elster and Miller.
39 DI 21.
40 ATP 213; original emphasis.
41 ATP 222.
42 One of the best is the following: "Were we to take the daily existence of any individual or follow up his career, we would always find that the satisfaction of all his needs, all interests, all desires, that is, of purposes, occurs in homes, in offices, in schools, in hospitals, on recreation grounds, in churches, in universities and research organization." Malinowski, *Freedom and Civilization*, p. 156.
43 Levi-Strauss, *Structural Anthropology*, p. 14.
44 Kant, *Anthropology*, p. 170.

45 See also Deleuze's discussion of this in KCP 73–5.
46 Freud 8.
47 Freud 7–8.
48 I&I 17.
49 See also Gregg Lambert's excellent discussion in *Who's Afraid*.
50 François Dosse has made this connection in a slightly different way (Dosse 225). His account also lucidly explains how and why Deleuze's rhetoric of "institutions" in the 50s gave way to Guattari's rhetoric of "groups" in the early 70s.
51 AO 342.
52 AO 26; original emphasis.
53 CC 112–15.
54 DR 96–128. Christian Kerslake makes this argument on similar grounds in *Deleuze and the Unconscious*.
55 And it would be remiss to not point out that in *Empiricism and Subjectivity* (1953), Deleuze was already working with a theory of temporal synthesis, one which took a form in *What is Grounding?* (1956) very close to the form Deleuze would put describe in *Difference and Repetition* (1968).
56 I intimated this in Chapter 2 above and explicitly argued for it in *Deleuze and the Genesis of Representation*.
57 AO 288.
58 AO 63; original emphasis.
59 "We define social formations by *machinic processes* and not by modes of production (these on the contrary depend on the processes)." ATP 435; original emphasis.
60 KA 81. An assemblage is produced when desire is folded into social formations.
61 AO 386n11.
62 Klossowski, *Nietzsche and the Vicious Circle*, 102; original emphases.
63 *Nietzsche and the Vicious Circle*, 101.
64 *Nietzsche and the Vicious Circle*, 103; original emphases.
65 Klossowski, *Such a Deathly Desire* p. 109.
66 DI 21.
67 AO 181.
68 NG 170.
69 AO 380.

70 AO 178.
71 Rawls, *Theory of Justice*, p. 293.
72 Patton 2000, 9. Nathan Jun endorses this view; see Jun 99.
73 May, 1994, 130, 133.
74 Esposito 194.
75 See Buchanan, "Desire and Ethics." Buchanan is not talking about Patton, May or Esposito in this piece, but rather Foucault.
76 The relevant passage, which I discussed above, is this: "Imagination is revealed as a veritable production of extremely diverse *models*: when drives (*les tendances*) are reflected in an imagination submitted to the principles of association, institutions are determined by the figures traced by the drives according to the circumstances." (ES 48).
77 See Chapter 2 above.

Bibliography

Badiou, A. (1999), *Deleuze: The Clamor of Being*, trans. L. Burchill, Minneapolis: University of Minnesota Press.
—(2004), *Theoretical Writings*, trans. R. Brassier and A. Toscano, New York: Continuum.
Bataille, G. (1997), *Choix de lettres: 1917–1962*, ed. M. Surya, Paris: Gallimard.
Beiser, F. C. (2002), *German Idealism: The Struggle against Subjectivism 1781–1801*, London: Harvard University Press.
Bell, J. (2009), *Deleuze's Hume: Philosophy, Culture and the Scottish Enlightenment*, Edinburgh: Edinburgh University Press.
Benjamin, W. (2004), *The Concept of Criticism in German Romanticism*, in *Walter Benjamin: Selected Writings Volume 1 1913–1926*, trans. D. Lachterman, H. Eiland, and I. Balfour, Cambridge, MA: Harvard University Press.
Bensmaïa, R. (2004), 'Cinéplastique: Gilles Deleuze lecteur d'Élie Faure', in *Cinéma, Art(s) Plastique(s)*, ed. P. Taminiaux and C. Murcia, Paris: L'Harmattan.
Bergson, H. (1991), *Matter and Memory*, trans. N. M. Paul and W. S. Palmer, New York: Zone Books.
—(1998), *Creative Evolution*, trans. A. Mitchell, Mineola, NY: Dover.
Blanchot, M. (1995), 'Literature and the Right to Death', trans. L. Davis, in *The Work of Fire*, trans. C. Mandell, Stanford: Stanford University Press.
Bowden, S. (2011), *The Priority of Events: Deleuze's Logic of Sense*, Edinburgh: Edinburgh University Press.
Broderick, A. (1970), 'Preface', in *The French Institutionalists: Maurice Hauriou, Georges Renard, Joseph T. Delos*, ed. A. Broderick, Cambridge, MA: Harvard University Press.
Bryant, L. (2008), *Difference and Giveness: Deleuze's Transcendental Empiricism and the Ontology of Immanence*, Evanston, IL: Northwestern University Press.
—(2011), 'The Ethics of the Event: Deleuze and Ethics without Arche', *Deleuze and Ethics*, ed. D. Smith and N. Jun, Edinburgh: Edinburgh University Press.
Buchanan, I. (2000), *Deleuzism: A Metacommentary*, Edinburgh: Edinburgh University Press.

—(2008), *Deleuze and Guattari's Anti-Oedipus*, New York: Continuum.
—(2011), 'Desire and Ethics', *Deleuze Studies*, 5 (supplement), 7–20.
Burke, E. (2004), *A Philosophical Enquiry into the Sublime and Beautiful and Other Pre-Revolutionary Writings*, New York: Penguin.
Canguilhem, G. (1962), *Besoins et tendances*, Paris: Hachette.
—(2009), *Knowledge of Life*, trans. D. Ginsbyrg and S. Geroulanos, New York: Fordham University Press.
Cavell, S. (1991), *Conditions Handsome and Unhandsome: The Constitution of Emersonian Perfectionism*, Chicago: University of Chicago Press.
Clark, T. (2008), 'Becoming Everyone: The Politics of Sympathy in Deleuze and Rorty', *Radical Philosophy*, 147 (Jan–Feb), 33–44.
Colebrook, C. (2002), *Gilles Deleuze*, New York: Routledge.
—(2010), *Deleuze and the Meaning of Life*, New York: Continuum.
Cressole, M. (1973), *Deleuze*, Paris: Éditions Universitaires.
Dejanovic, S. (2011), 'The Creative Power of Desire: A Brief Genealogy from Kant to Deleuze'. Creation, Crisis, Critique: The Fourth International Deleuze Studies Conference, Copenhagen Business School. 27 June 2011. Conference Presentation.
DeLanda, M. (2005), *Intensive Science and Virtual Philosophy*, New York: Continuum.
Deleuze, G. (1953), *Instincts et institutions*, Paris: Hachette.
—(1985), *Cinéma 2: l'Image-temps*, Paris: Les Éditions de Minuit.
—(1986), *Cinema 1: The Movement-Image*, trans. H. Tomlinson and R. Galeta, Minneapolis: University of Minnesota Press.
—(1988a), *Foucault*, trans. S. Hand, Minneapolis: University of Minnesota Press.
—(1988b), *Spinoza: Practical Philosophy*, trans. R. Hurley, San Francisco, CA: City Lights Books.
—(1989), *Cinema 2: The Time-Image*, trans. H. Tomlinson and R. Galeta, Minneapolis: University of Minnesota Press.
—(1990), *The Logic of Sense*, trans. M. Lester and C. Stivale, ed. C. Boundas, New York: Columbia University Press.
—(1991a), *Bergsonism*, trans. H. Tomlinson and B. Habberjam, New York: Zone Books.
—(1991b), *Empiricism and Subjectivity: And Essay on Hume's theory of Human Nature*, trans. C. Boundas, New York: Columbia University Press.
—(1992), *Expressionism in Philosophy: Spinoza*, trans. M. Joughin, New York: Zone Books.
—(1994), *Difference and Repetition*, trans. P. Patton, New York: Columbia University Press.
—(1995), *Negotiations 1972–1990*, trans. M. Joughin, New York: Columbia University Press.

—(2000), *Proust and Signs*, trans. R. Howard, Minneapolis: University of Minnesota Press.
—(2001), *Pure Immanence: Essays on A Life*, trans. A. Boyman, New York: Zone Books.
—(2006), *Nietzsche and Philosophy*, trans. H. Tomlinson, New York: Columbia University Press.
—(2007), 'Pericles and Verdi', in *Dialogues II*, trans. J. Hughes and V. Robinson, New York: Columbia University Press, pp. 153–65.
Deleuze, G. and F. Guattari (1994), *What is Philosophy?*, trans. H. Tomlinson and G. Burchell, New York: Columbia University Press.
Dickens, C. (2009), *Our Mutual Friend*, New York: Oxford University Press.
Dosse, F. (2011), *Gilles Deleuze and Felix Guattari: Intersecting Lives*, New York: Columbia University Press.
Elster, J. (1989), *Nuts and Bolts for the Social Sciences*, New York: Cambridge University Press.
Esposito, R. (2008), *Bios: Biopolitics and Philosophy*, trans. T. Campbell, Minneapolis: University of Minnesota Press.
Foucault, M. (1977), 'Theatrum Philosophicum', in *Language, Counter-Memory, Practice: Selected Interviews and Essays*, ed. and trans. D. F. Bouchard, Ithaca, NY: Cornell University Press.
—(2002), *The Order of Things*, London: Routledge.
—(2008), *Introduction to Kant's* Anthropology, trans. R. Nigro and K. Briggs, Los Angeles, CA: Semiotext(e).
Freud, S. (1961), *The Future of an Illusion*, trans. J. Strachey, New York: Norton.
Gasché, R. (2003), *The Idea of Form: Rethinking Kant's Aesthetics*, Stanford: Stanford University Press.
Gatens, M. and G. Lloyd (1999), *Collective Imaginings: Spinoza, Past and Present*, New York: Routledge.
Ginsborg, H. (1997), 'Lawfulness without Law: Kant on the Free Play of Imagination and Understanding', *Philosophical Topics*, 25: 37–81.
Guéroult, M. (1930), *L'evolution et structure de la doctrine de la science chez Fichte*, 2 vols, Paris: Belles Lettres.
Guyer, P. (1979), *Kant and the Claims of Taste*, Cambridge, MA: Harvard University Press.
—(2005), *Values of Beauty: Historical Essays in Aesthetics*, New York: Cambridge University Press.
—(2011), 'Kantian Perfectionism', *Perfecting Virtue: New Essays on Kantian Ethics and Virtue Ethics*, ed. L. Jost and J. Wuerth, New York: Cambridge University Press.
Hallward, P. (2006), *Out of this World: Deleuze and the Philosophy of Creation*, New York: Verso.
Hardt, M. (1993), *Gilles Deleuze: An Apprenticeship in Philosophy*, Minneapolis: University of Minnesota Press.

Heidegger, M. (1992), *History of the Concept of Time*, Bloomington, IN: Indiana University Press.
Hughes, J. (2009), *Deleuze and the Genesis of Representation*, New York: Continuum.
—(2010a), 'Believing in the Word: Toward an Ethics of Form', in *Deleuze and the Body*, Edinburgh: Edinburgh University Press.
—(2010b), *Deleuze's Difference and Repetition*, New York: Continuum.
Hume, D. (1994), *Political Essays*, ed. K. Haakonssen, New York: Cambridge University Press.
Hyppolite, J. (1974), *Genesis and Structure of Hegel's Phenomenology of Spirit*, trans. S. Cherniak and J. Heckman, Evanston, IL: Northwestern University Press.
Jun, N. (2011), 'Deleuze, Values, and Normativity', in *Deleuze and Ethics*, ed. D. Smith and N. Jun, Edinburgh: Edinburgh University Press.
Kant, I. (1992), *Lectures on Logic*, trans. M. Young, New York: Cambridge University Press.
—(1993a), *Critique of Practical Reason*, trans. L. W. Beck, New Jersey: Prentice-Hall.
—(1993b), *Opus postumum*, trans. E. Forster and M. Rosen, New York: Cambridge University Press.
—(1996), *The Metaphysics of Morals*, trans. M. Gregor, New York: Cambridge University Press.
—(1998), *Critique of Pure Reason*, trans. P. Guyer and A. Wood, New York: Cambridge University Press.
—(2000a), *Critique of the Power of Judgment*, trans. P. Guyer and E. Matthews, New York: Cambridge University Press.
—(2000b), *Groundwork of The Metaphysics of Morals*, trans. H. J. Paton, London: Routledge.
—(2007), *Anthropology* in *Anthropology, History and Education*, trans. R. B. Louden, New York: Cambridge University Press.
Kaufman, E. (2001), *The Delirium of Praise: Bataille, Blanchot, Deleuze Foucault, Klossowski*, Baltimore, MD: Johns Hopkins University Press.
Kerslake, C. (2007), *Deleuze and the Unconscious*, London: Continuum.
—(2009), *Immanence and the Vertigo of Philosophy: From Kant to Deleuze*, Edinburgh: Edinburgh University Press.
—(2010), 'Deleuze and the Dialectics of Love: Deleuze, Canguilhelm, and the Philosophy of Desire', in *Deleuze and Psychoanalysis*, ed. L. de Bolle, Leuven: Leuven University Press.
Kisner, M. (2011), *Spinoza on Human Freedom: Reason, Autonomy and the Good Life*, Cambridge: Cambridge University Press.
Klossowski, P. (2005), *Nietzsche and the Vicious Circle*, trans. D. Smith, New York: Continuum.
—(2007), *Such a Deathly Desire*, trans. R. Ford, Albany: SUNY Press.

Lacan, J. (1992), *The Ethics of Psychoanalysis 1959–1960*, ed. J.-A. Miller, trans. D. Porter, New York: Norton.
—(1998), *The Four Fundamental Concepts of Psychoanalysis*, ed. J.-A. Miller, trans. A. Sheridan, New York: Norton.
Lambert, G. (2008), *Who's Afraid of Deleuze and Guattari*, New York: Continuum.
Lecercle, J.-J. (1996), 'The Pedagogy of Philosophy', *Radical Philosophy* 75 (Jan–Feb), 44–6.
Le Coeur, C. (1939), *Le Rite etl'outil: Essaisur le rationalism social et la pluralité des civilizations*, Paris: PUF Alcan.
Lefebvre, A. (2008), *The Image of Law: Deleuze, Bergson, Spinoza*, Stanford: Stanford University Press.
Levi-Strauss, C. (1963), *Structural Anthropology*, trans. C. Jacobson and B. Schoepf, New York: Basic Books.
Longueness, B. (2001), *Kant and the Capacity to Judge: Sensibility and Discursivity in the Transcendental Analytic*, Princeton, NJ: Princeton University Press.
Macherey, P. (1996), 'The Encounter with Spinoza', in *Deleuze: A Critical Reader*, ed. P. Patton, Oxford: Blackwell.
Makkreel, R. (1990), *Imagination and Interpretation in Kant: The Hermeneutical Import of the Critique of Judgment*, Chicago: University of Chicago Press.
Malinowski, B. (1947), *Freedom and Civilization*, London: Allan Wingate.
—(1953), *Sex and Repression in Savage Society*, London: Routledge and Kegan Paul.
Marrati, P. (2001), 'The Catholicism of Cinema: Gilles Deleuze on Image and Belief', in *Religion and Media*, ed. H. de Vries and S. Weber, Stanford: Stanford University Press.
—(2008), *Gilles Deleuze: Cinema and Philosophy*, trans. A. Hartz, Baltimore, MD: The Johns Hopkins University Press.
May, T. (2005), *Gilles Deleuze: An Introduction*, New York: Cambridge University Press.
Meillassoux, Q. (2010), *After Finitude*, trans. R. Brassier, New York: Continuum.
Merleau-Ponty, M. (2002), *Phenomenology of Perception*, London: Routledge.
Miller, S. (2010), *The Moral Foundations of Social Institutions*, New York: Cambridge University Press.
Moulard-Leonard, V. (2009), *Bergson-Deleuze Encounters: Transcendental Experience and the Thought of the Virtual*, Albany: SUNY Press.
Patron, S. (1999), *Critique 1946–1996: Une encylcopédie de l'esprit moderne*, Paris: Éditions de L'IMEC.
Patton, P. (2000), *Deleuze and the Political*, New York: Routledge.

—(2010), *Deleuzian Concepts: Philosophy, Colonization, Politics,* Stanford: Stanford University Press.
Peterson, K. R. (2004), 'Translator's Introduction', in F. W. J. Schelling's *First Outline of a System of the Philosophy of Nature,* trans. K. R. Peterson, Albany: SUNY Press.
Pisters, P. (2003), *The Matrix of Visual Culture: Working with Deleuze in Film Theory,* Stanford: Stanford University Press.
Protevi, J. (2001), 'The Organism as the Judgment of God: Aristotle, Kant and Deleuze on Nature (that is, on Biology, Theology and Politics)', in *Deleuze and Religion,* ed. M. Bryden, New York: Routledge.
—(2009), *Political Affect: Connecting the Social and Somatic,* Minneapolis: University of Minnesota Press.
Rawls, J. (1999), *A Theory of Justice (Revised Edition),* Cambridge, MA: Harvard University Press.
Rodowick, D. N. (1997), *Gilles Deleuze's Time Machine,* Durham, NC: Duke University Press.
Roger, P. (2006), 'Critique' in *The Columbia History of Twentieth-Century French Thought,* ed. L. Kritzman, New York: Columbia University Press.
Rossellini, R. (1985), *The War Trilogy: Open City, Paisan, Germany—Year Zero,* trans. J. Green, New York: Garland Publishing.
Rothfield, P. (2011), 'Dance and the Passing Moment' in *Deleuze and the Body,* ed. L. Guillaume and J. Hughes, Edinburgh: Edinburgh University Press.
Rousseau, J.-J. (1979), *Emile or On Education,* trans, A. Bloom, New York: Basic Books.
—(2010a), *The Discourses and Other Early Political Writings,* trans. V. Gourevitch, New York: Cambridge University Press.
—(2010b), *The Social Contract and Other Later Political Writings,* New York: Cambridge University Press.
Sauvagnargues, A. (2009), *Deleuze: L'Empirisme transcendental,* Paris: PUF.
Spinoza, B. (1992), *Ethics,* trans. S. Shirley, ed. S. Feldman, Indianapolis: Hackett.
Surya, M. (2010), *Georges Bataille: An Intellectual Biography,* London: Verso.
Vogler, C. (2002), *Reasonably Vicious,* Cambridge, MA: Harvard University Press.
Welchman, A. (2009), 'Deleuze's Post-Critical Metaphysics', *Symposium,* 13.2, 25–54.
Zabunyan, D. (2006), *Gilles Deleuze: Voir, parler, penser au risque du cinéma,* Paris: Presses Sorbonne Nouvelle.

Index

Alain 134
aleatory point 44–50, 90–1, 93–4, 151nn. 58–9, 152nn. 60–1
animal, the 20, 70, 77, 79, 101, 106, 108, 129–30, 136
Antonioni, M. 89
apprehension 16, 35, 41–2, 64, 66, 70, 85, 95, 102, 158n. 14
Aristotle 94
Artaud, A. 91
attitude 88, 92–4, 129, 131

Bacon, F. 41–2, 81–2, 95, 110, 113
Badiou, A. 13–17, 21, 24, 81
Bataille, G. 8
Beckett, S. 86
Bell, J. 139
Bergson, H. 6, 23, 36–8, 48–50, 74–5, 83–95, 119, 123, 124–5, 127–9, 158n. 8
Blanchot, M. 4, 8–9, 49
body 37–8, 46, 52–3, 58–67, 83–95, 100–1, 110–11, 129–31, 133
body without organs 36–9, 59–60, 107–8, 140
Bryant, L. 71–2, 90
Burke, E. 100

Canguilhem, G. 124–6, 149n. 52
Cavell, S. 77, 153n. 3

Claudel, P. 8
cliché 41–2, 55–6, 80, 95, 146
cogito 30, 44–7
counter-actualization 90
Cressole, M. 5, 7, 101
culture 58, 61–2, 76–7, 80, 108, 129–31, 136, 157n. 56

DeLanda, M. 24
Derrida, J. 148n. 23
Descartes, R. 30
Dickens, C. 47
Duras, M. 86

Emerson, R. W. 77
Esposito, R. 144, 146

finitude 28–31, 34, 39, 50, 74, 151n. 40, 152n. 173
Foucault, M. 6, 77, 99, 107, 150n. 21, 152n. 73, 160n. 47
Frazer, J. 134
Freud, S. 37, 70, 125–8, 135–7, 140

Garrel, P. 92
Giordias, M. 9
Godard, J.-L. 94
Groethuysen, B. 138

habit 4–5, 9, 25, 36, 38, 42, 53, 71, 88, 90, 122
Hairou, M. 124–5
Hardt, M. 114
Hegel, G. W. F. 25–6, 30, 31

INDEX

Heidegger, M. 31, 77
Hume, D. 5, 6, 28, 31, 36, 92, 119–42
Husserl, E. 32
institutions 8–9, 114–15, 119–46, 163n. 19

Kafka, F. 19–20, 110
Kant, I. 1, 5, 7, 8, 27–31, 32–5, 41–5, 50–3, 60, 67–8, 70–3, 81, 96–111, 135–6
Kaufman, E. 147–8n. 21
Kazan, E. 86
Kerslake, C. 27, 126
Klossowski, P. 6, 9, 54, 141–2, 145

Lacan, J. 126, 134
Le Coeur, C. 131
Leibniz, G. W. 12–13, 22, 28, 48, 50
Levi-Strauss, C. 124, 134–5
life 34, 47–9, 57, 61, 73–5, 81, 94, 96–108, 126–8, 144, 146
Linnaeus 86

Macherey, P. 22, 76–7
Malinowski, B. 124, 129–34, 137
Mallarmé, S. 8
Marrati, P. 86, 110–11
May, T. 144, 146
Meillassoux, Q. 30, 44
Merleau-Ponty, M. 28, 32, 150n. 7

Nietzsche, F. 5–7, 10, 20, 26, 30, 36, 57, 69–75, 81, 97–8

Panther, P. 19
Parnet, C. 20
Patton, P. 144, 146

plasticity 34, 38, 55, 59–62, 69, 72–3, 106–7, 112, 155n. 59
Plato 27
Plekhanov, G. 135, 137
posture *see* attitude
Proust, M. 28, 80–1, 95–6, 110

Rawls, J. 144, 157n. 96
recognition 35, 41–5, 65, 70–1, 74, 86–92, 95, 158n. 14
reproduction 35, 39, 41, 64, 66, 70, 85–6, 95, 158n. 14
Resnais, A. 91
Rilke, R. M. 8
Rossellini, R. 89
Rousseau, J.-J. 115–19, 136, 138, 163nn. 7–8

Snow, M. 86
soul 15, 62–5, 102–8, 158–9n. 20
Spinoza, B. 5, 11–13, 22, 28, 37, 47–8, 57–69, 73–5, 94, 97–8, 111, 144
style 1–26, 42
Surya, M. 8
synthesis 15–16, 23–4, 26, 32–5, 38–41, 60, 63–4, 69–70, 85–6, 95 140–2

territorialization 18–19, 23–4, 53, 79, 112, 122, 144–5
thought (faculty of) 1–3, 15, 25, 34–5, 41–5, 69–75, 90–1, 94, 145, 152n. 61

Vertov, D. 86

Welles, O. 86, 90–1, 94

www.ingramcontent.com/pod-product-compliance
Lightning Source LLC
Chambersburg PA
CBHW052047300426
44117CB00012B/2007